L e a d i n g s

Leadings

A Catholic's Journey through Quakerism

Irene Lape

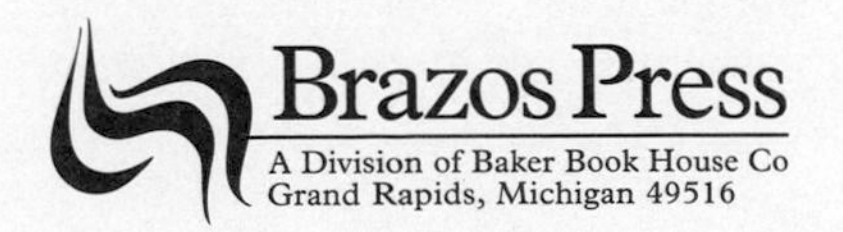
Brazos Press
A Division of Baker Book House Co
Grand Rapids, Michigan 49516

Published by Brazos Press
a division of Baker Book House Company
P.O. Box 6287, Grand Rapids, MI 49516-6287

Printed in the United States of America

Library of Congress Cataloging-in-Publication Data

Lape, Irene, 1945-
Leadings : a Catholic's journey through Quakerism / Irene Lape.
p. cm.
Includes bibliographical references.
ISBN 1-58743-054-1
1. Lape, Irene, 1945- 2. Catholic converts—United States—Biography. 3. Ex-church members—Society of Friends—Biography. 4. Society of Friends—Relations—Catholic Church. 5. Catholic Church—Relations—Society of Friends. 6. Society of Friends—Doctrines. 7. Catholic Church—Doctrines. I. Title
BX4668.L37 A3 2003
282′.092—dc21 2002013532

For current information about all releases from Brazos Press, visit our web site:
http://www.brazospress.com

Contents

Introduction

God does not enter our lives without leaving a story behind, and the story God leaves is not just any story; it is the story that somehow defines who we are, what we were created to be, and what our life has really been about. This is my story. Like most such stories, it is deeply entangled with the particulars of my life. I don't really think these particulars are all that significant, but we are interested in them today perhaps more than people in other historical eras, so I have included a good many of them. The outward events of my life are also a lot like those of most of my contemporaries, but one of the most important lessons I learned in coming to recognize God in my life is how similar the core of the story is to the stories of people even in the distant past. Everybody's story moves along a similar trajectory. Mine is a story of conversion—different kinds of conversion or maybe different stages of one ongoing and deepening conversion.

I have several reasons for sharing my story at such length. One is just to reflect and give praise to God for his great patience and love for me. When I look back on my life, I have a sense that I was caught in his net pretty early on; I tried hard to slip out at a certain point, and I might have had it not been for an extra measure of his grace. I also share my story to recognize and give thanks to those in my life who were unique channels of God's grace to me—my grandparents, who at a time in their lives when they should have been able to just rest and retire, having raised five children of their own, stepped back into the thankless task of childrearing when I needed them; and my dearest friend and husband, whose centrality to my story is not adequately acknowledged by these allusive references. He understands as no one else I have ever met that religion is lived out on the ground, in the concrete details of our lives.

My story is very ecumenical. I had no firm religious home from which to start out, and no one tradition has shaped the road I have traveled. I was baptized as a child into the Episcopal Church, made the decision in college to join the Catholic Church, lost my faith in God not long after that, and only found my way back because my faith was revived through an encounter with early Quaker Christianity. Today I am a Catholic again, but I am not here to trumpet the spiritual supremacy of any one tradition. I have reasons to be back that I think are compelling, but I hope that what my story reveals is God's ubiquitous presence and the grace that draws us to him. The great obstacles to faith in my life have been the idols of modernity—radical secularism, philosophical materialism, and political ideology—idols that seem compelling and convincing in many ways. But my experience and my testimony is that these idols can never explain or give expression to the deepest realities of our existence as human beings. For this we must turn back to the great God of Abraham, Isaac, and Jacob, who is present for us in Christ.

There is yet another purpose in my writing this account of my religious journey: to seek a discerning response to the insights and openings I think I have been given. I say "I think" because the more I reflect on God—his unimaginable transcendence—and on the insurmountable limitations under which we human beings operate, the more I realize how little I can ever say for sure about him. This is about faith, not scientific knowledge, but it seems a necessary faith to me, and scientific knowledge will never answer the needs of our deepest nature. One of the great insights of Quaker Christians is that God continues to reveal his reality and his truth to those who join themselves to him in faith, and perhaps because I have been so shaped by Friends, I have come to see the things God has opened to me in my journey as things I am asked to share and lay before the believing community for their review and prayerful consideration. I am not a religious scholar, but I think the dialogue about faith and the truth it penetrates must go on among all of us—those trained in philosophy, religious doctrine, and history, biblical scholars, and even those of us who are "only" believers.

The vision I offer is at heart a plea for unity. I hope that Catholics who read my story may find in the message and spirituality of Friends an approach to the gospel that is both challenging and complementary to the faith they hold and practice; it is also my hope that Friends who read it might find their way back to the outward testimonies and forms that I believe are necessary to sustain the gospel truths on which their vision rests. And as for those who do not believe—as I did not for so many years—I hope that if they read my story they too might find in it a way around the barriers our secular and skeptical world erects to separate them from the profound truths and rewards religious faith attempts to penetrate and make available to us. We are one human creation. God seeks us for his own, that we might have the life he offers to us in all its fullness.

1

Home Is Where One Starts From

When I look back on my life and the lives of the people who brought me into the world and raised me, it is amazing to me that I ever came to be a Christian. My parents were both atheists—atheists of the Marxist persuasion. They were militantly and ideologically atheistic in their views. For them, religion was a relic of humanity's prescientific efforts to understand and explain the universe and the world in which they had to survive. It may have been necessary or done some good in its day, but it had also been the source of most of the oppression and conflict in history. In the modern world, with what science and reason could open to us about the nature of reality, it was irrational for anyone to believe in it. The institutions that advanced it were wedded to societal and economic interests that were reactionary and oppressive. It was the job of all enlightened people to unmask, discredit, and overthrow all these interests and institutions.

I was born to this couple in September of 1945, a month after the first atomic bomb was dropped on Hiroshima. I was their second child. Their first, another daughter, had been born nine years earlier. In that nine years, they had moved to Hawaii to help organize pineapple workers, my father had joined the navy to fight fascism, and the marriage had soured to the point of separation. My mother had never been a very good match for my father; he was too intellectual for her. She tried to be as good a Marxist as he was, as cerebral and radical, but she was just not up to it by nature. He made everyone around him want to be as good a Marxist as he was—his mother, his sister, his daughters. He was charismatic in that way. I was supposed to have been a new start for my parents—an inspiration to overcome the difficulties they had experienced together—but I didn't work. By the time I was a year old, my father had left the family for good to go to New York City and finish the academic requirements he needed to set up practice as a psychiatric social worker. In 1947, my parents divorced. Soon after, my father remarried—a professional woman this time, also in the field of psychology and more nearly his intellectual equal. Within a year or two there was another family of daughters to care for.

My mother stayed on where she and my father had lived before marrying, the town of Bronxville, New York, just outside New York City. Both her parents and my father's parents still lived there, and I think it was around the time of the divorce that my mother started leaving me with her parents. I was two. She and my father went out to Reno, Nevada, to settle things—that was what you did in those days. Reno was the only place where you could get a no-fault divorce quickly and easily. I don't know what my mother's state of mind was at the time, but apparently she had a brief affair with a man out there once the divorce was final, an affair that led to a pregnancy and an abortion in fairly short order. I don't know how long she stayed in Nevada or any other details about this unhappy episode. She told me about it many years later, a year or so before she died, but I believed it. It apparently formed the foundation of a paranoid obsession that grew in her over the next ten years, an obsession that would ultimately lead to her hospitalization for schizophrenia. No one saw it at the time, however—not her parents, not even her psychiatrically savvy ex-husband.

In any case, I was with my maternal grandparents while all of this was going on. Upon my mother's return from Nevada, she moved to New York City and got an apartment on the lower East Side and a job working at Macy's department store. I don't know how many times I visited her there, but it must have been at least a few, enough to permit me to remember a feature or two about the place and its environs—like the brass fire hydrant that protruded from the side of an apartment building we passed on the way to Washington Square Park, which was not far away. But mostly my mother visited me out in the suburbs.

My sister, eleven at the time of the divorce, was the one who bore the brunt of my parents' breakup and my mother's slide into mental illness. My mother used to send her to the park, where there were frequent art shows, and tell her to inspect the paintings on the street for messages. The man she had known—the mysterious Nevada man—was supposed to be sending her a coded message embedded in a painting, telling her when he would be coming for her. My sister tried to leave her, tried to go live with our father and his new family, but there were problems there as well: problems fitting in, sharing him with his new family, feeling at home. So she flitted back and forth for two or three years until she finally found a family that took her in to babysit their children in return for room and board. By this time—early adolescence—my sister also had problems that made her somewhat difficult to be around; it is impossible, therefore, to say with any certainty where the problems everyone had with one another were rooted. It always amazed me that my father, who was the most careful observer of life I have ever known and a trained psychologist—not to speak of his new wife who was also a psychologist—never saw the nascent schizophrenia with which both my mother and sister were afflicted. My mother would succumb a few years later, around the age of thirty-eight, and spend most of her life in the state psychiatric system; my sister would succumb in middle age as well after many years of struggling with less acute forms of neurosis.

I don't think there was ever a day on which it was decided that I would stay with my grandparents. It just seemed to happen. Or maybe it was part of some plan in the mind of God. I don't know. I am only profoundly grateful that things worked out for me as they did. The fact that I didn't live with my parents, however, doesn't mean that I didn't experience their influence. I saw both my father and mother—and my sister—on a fairly regular basis and knew they cared for me. When my father came out to visit with me, we would do fun things together—go to see a movie or go to the zoo, visit a local amusement park where there was an ice-skating rink in the winter. My favorite thing to do was go horseback riding, so we often did that—I would ride and he would watch and comment. Later, when I did start traveling to the city to see him, we would go to the Natural History Museum or the planetarium or a show. Whatever we did, we always talked—that is what I mostly remember about the visits I had with my father. We talked about everything. He was a believer in science and in knowledge, and he believed that the "meaningful life" was the life dedicated to understanding things as they were and to changing the world we lived in according to our best knowledge of it. He marveled at the universe and the history of man. He believed in our power to comprehend it and shape it to our highest ideals.

I don't remember as well the things I did with my mother. I did visit her and my sister several times in my mother's apartment in the city. I never visited my father's home or met his second family until I was nearly nine years old. I had a few interesting memories of my mother's place—taking enormous bubble baths, watching the toaster in the kitchen pop toast out the window into a courtyard below, visiting Washington Square Park nearby. I don't think I ever felt during these early years that my parents didn't love me or that I was weird in any way. I just didn't live with them. I never saw them asleep or rummaging around the house in their pajamas. I never sat on my father's lap or had either of them read to me or tell me stories or "veg out" with me in front of the television. I never had the opportunity to get mad at them for bossing me around or being unreasonable in the way parents are always unreasonable to their kids—all the things ordinary kids take for granted. Peace and pleasantness reigned almost all the time when I was with my parents because we only saw each other now and then, as visitors in each other's lives. When I was about eight, I would go through a period of painful self-consciousness about the strangeness of my family situation, and later in adolescence I would go through an even deeper dejection, especially in relation to my father whom I loved and admired very much. But not in these early years. I was all right with things then. I was happy. It didn't occur to me until many years later how positively blessed I had been to have been given some distance from my parents in my childhood. It helped me see that I could be different from them—live a different life from them, embrace different values, believe in and do different things.

Everything about the grandparents I lived with was different from my parents—more conventional. They were happy together and loved each other deeply. They were interested in the world, but they were not intellectuals. We didn't talk about every little thing, every little idea the way I did with my father. My grandmother—Ni Ni—was a quietly devout woman, a Catholic and a "lady" raised in a well-to-do family in Trinidad. She took me to church with her, taught me to say my prayers each night kneeling on my bed—the Our Father, the Hail Mary, and blessings on everyone in the family. She didn't talk to me about religion that I can remember, but she gave me habits of faith I would not forget. All the little objects of devotion I would associate with my grandparents' home—the wooden crucifix that hung on our wall, the blue rosary beads my grandmother used, the tiny relic she had (a single thread purportedly taken from the floor of the room in which St. Teresa of Lisieux died, framed with a picture of the saint)—were hers. My grandfather—Dumps—was an all-American Horatio Alger type, born in New York City and raised in modest surroundings. As a very young man, without college degree or family connections, he was personally recruited by W. R. Grace to work in his company, and he rose to success in it, importing cocoa from Central and South America. In 1929, he left and formed his own import business—just in time to get hit by the Great Depression. The Depression was the event around which my grandfather's life could be organized. He never recovered from it economically or psychologically. After paying off the men who had invested in his company in 1929 and salting away a little to live on, he never really worked again after 1930. Maybe that's why when I came along he saw caring for me as his vocation.

My grandfather was the main caregiver and parent figure in my life. He was utterly and completely devoted to me. He was the one who drew my bath and put me to bed, the one who read to me or told me stories, the one I could send off at bedtime to go get me an ice cream downtown or count to a million for me if I was having trouble getting to sleep. He was the one who hauled me on my sled through the snow and told me all the family stories—about the great-great-grandfather who had been a soldier in Stonewall Jackson's army, and the great-grandfather who had been a deputy marshal in Abilene, Kansas, and known

Buffalo Bill Cody, about his having been "king of the hill" when Cody's Wild West Show came to New York City and he was invited to sit in a box seat. Religiously, I guess he was what you would call lapsed Catholic. He had been an altar boy in his youth and a practicing Catholic as a young adult, but he had stopped going to church when a priest during the Depression had had the audacity to criticize his hero (Franklin Delano Roosevelt) in a homily. My grandfather never went back. His real religion was centered around Roosevelt and the patriotic liberal Americanism Roosevelt articulated for a generation of Americans traumatized by economic depression, war, and ideological conflict.

These were my worlds—the worlds I would have to negotiate as I got older and faced the questions of what I believed and what I wanted my own life to be: the rather conventional religious and civic world of my grandparents on one side, and on the other side the more intellectually "modern" world of my parents and older sister, with their belief in Marxism, their faith in science and psychology to explain and overcome human problems, and their cynicism toward capitalism and American government generally.

The world I lived in with my grandparents was not inhabited by us alone. For the first few years we lived alone, but when I was about four we moved in with an uncle (my mother's brother), his wife, and their young son, who was six years older than I. I think the reason must have been economic, but there may also have been a thought to giving me a more "normal" family situation and perhaps some security in the event my grandparents were to die or become incapacitated. Religiously, my uncle and aunt were very nominally Catholic; and while they attended church weekly, they were very poor models of Catholic religiosity. They drank too much and argued too much. Things were never really happy when we all were together, but we succeeded pretty much in living to ourselves. My grandmother took me to church with her; the rest of the family went to a different Mass. We didn't function much as a whole. After three to four years of trying to make a go of it as a family together, my grandparents decided to bail out. They found an apartment in a nearby town, and the three of us moved. It was in this new town that God first became important to me.

I have no memory of any personal sense of God in my life before we moved when I was in the middle of the third grade. I said my prayers at night as instructed. I went to church. I gave up things for a few days every Lent, but I have no memory of any special feelings or thoughts of God until after our move, when life started to get complicated.

The first thing that happened was my mother came to get me. It couldn't have been more than a day after we moved in that she arrived unexpectedly, saying she wanted me to come with her—not for a visit but to stay. Later I would learn that she came in part because my sister (then seventeen) had left her in anger the night before, this time for good. She came for me with a look on her face I had never seen, a look that made me recoil from her and seek refuge on the back of our living room couch. She accused my grandparents of trying to take me from her. She reached out to pull me down, but I evaded her. My grandparents pleaded with her to leave. I pleaded with her. I tried to reason with her, to assure her I would visit her sometime soon—just not now. School was starting Monday. She followed me around the room as I climbed from one piece of furniture to another, talking with her, staying just out of her reach. What I remember most vividly was the split in me: the inside feelings, terrified and determined not to go; the outside words, calm and eager to show I cared. I wanted to come, my mouth said, just not now. I did want to be with her, I lied, just not all the time. Finally, my grandfather called my uncle on the telephone to ask him to come and help with her. What that might have signified to my mother I do not know, but she left as suddenly as she had come.

Later that night, I learned years later, back in her apartment in the city, she broke down completely. She locked herself in her apartment, believing her "enemies" were out to get her—the Nevada man she had waited for but who had never come, the New York governor he was friends with, and others they had brought with them. They were outside her apartment waiting to kill her. She called her therapist. He convinced her to go to a psychiatric ward and commit herself. The next time I saw her (two years later) she was at a state psychiatric hospital in Wingdale, New York. She would remain there or in a rest home for the rest of her life.

Six months after these events, my grandmother died. I woke up one morning and her bed, next to mine, was empty, still made from the day before. She had suffered a heart attack the night before, after I had gone to bed. She was in a hospital, but I couldn't visit her. Children were not permitted in those days to visit in hospitals. On Thanksgiving Day 1954, she died. My grandfather thought it would be too upsetting for me to go to the funeral, so I didn't go. I stayed at home. I never saw her sick or dead or buried. She was just gone.

Suddenly life seemed like a house of cards—fragile and unstable, with walls tumbling in and things coming down all around me. My grandmother was gone. My mother was ill and hospitalized. My grandfather seemed older to me than he had seemed before, and old I knew now was something very bad. He talked about being old and pitiful—"Poor old Dumpsie," he would say. And there were other things afoot as well. I overheard people—family or friends or neighbors (I don't remember who)—talking about the possibility of placing me in an orphanage. Was it then that my father decided I should meet my stepmother and half-sisters? Did they think of taking me in? I'm not sure. I only know that suddenly life was full of turns I could not foresee, and I was afraid. I couldn't go to sleep at night without singing to myself to avoid thinking. I couldn't look out the window for fear of the searchlight that swept the night sky over the town where we lived. When I woke in the morning I froze, thinking that my grandfather might not be in the other room. Maybe he was only fooling me about being old. Maybe he just wore an old-face mask. What would I do if he died?

I prayed. I prayed in a more serious and personal way than I had ever prayed before. I remember one night in particular, praying into the dark and starry sky over a street near where I lived, that God would not take Dumps from me until he was ninety-four. I could bear it then, but not before. That prayer was a small thing, but it brought a feeling of release and reassurance that I had never experienced before. God would not let him die. I stopped worrying about whether his face was real or not.

But death was not the only thing I worried about. I started to fret over the peculiarities of my family situation—the fact that I had to visit my parents, the fact that my mother was in a hospital and had "something wrong with her head," the fact that I lived with my grandfather. I started making things up about my life, lying to my friends about what was going on. I told them my parents were in Vermont on a huge, beautiful horse farm that they needed to watch over and that I lived with my grandfather because there were no good schools there. I put up a picture of a farm in my room and pretended that was our farm. I spent my summers there. I made up all kinds of embellishments to the story, but that was the core of it. It wasn't long before I was afraid to bring anyone home to our apartment for fear they would learn I was lying to them all the time.

In the midst of these events and anxieties, I was baptized into the Episcopal Church. My grandmother had never had me baptized. My parents would never have permitted it. The Catholic Church was the epitome of everything they hated in religion. When we moved to Yonkers, however, we moved near another aunt of mine (my mother's younger sister). It was she who approached my grandfather about having me baptized. She thought I needed some kind of regular religious life—a church to go to, a community to be part of, a Sunday school where I could learn about God and Jesus. She, like my mother, had been raised a Catholic, but she had left over some issue and joined the Episcopal Church. She went with her children and didn't mind picking me up to go with them. So it was decided. I didn't choose it or think about it at all, but I remember walking down the aisle of the crowded church to the baptismal font near the front. I remember feeling the water on my head and hearing the priest asking what name I was to have.

A few months after this, however, Dumps and I moved again—back in with my uncle and his family. This move, like the earlier one, was a turning point in my life, but this time a good and treasured one, one that brought me close to God and really laid the foundation of everything that was to happen to me later on.

2

The Parts of the Puzzle

From the day we moved to the new house my uncle had found for us to live in, God moved to the very center of my life and consciousness. The house stood on the grounds of a great old estate that had been built by a relative of Alexander Hamilton. There was a huge white mansion at the top of a long sloping hill near the front of the estate. We didn't live in that. We lived in what must have been the caretaker's cottage, just north of it. The "cottage" was actually very large and formed a semi-circle around a spacious courtyard, off of which there were stables and kennels built into the lower level of the building. We were in one of four apartments that had been created out of the cottage. Our part of the dwelling alone had four bedrooms, two baths, a large living room, a dining room, and a kitchen. The other apartments were smaller. The estate was owned by a man who lived in one of these. He used the estate as a summer day camp for New York City youngsters. There was an outdoor swimming pool behind the mansion, apple orchards, a formal garden, heavy-duty playground equipment like swings and slides and merry-go-rounds, and maybe thirty acres of fields and lawns. Had I tried to imagine such a place as this, I would not have been able to—it was so different from anything I had ever known. Best of all, there were stables with room for five or six horses, and a zoo (a converted greenhouse) with animals that were used as a part of the camp program in summer and as a resource for children's television in the winters. The woman who ran this zoo often appeared on the well-known children's show *Captain Kangaroo* with her baby orangutan, BoBo. It was a fabulous place and I loved every square inch of it.

The first night I spent in this new house was a night I will never forget. When I woke up the next morning, I would have a completely new start to my life, and I knew the lying had to stop. In as solemn a moment as I have ever had in my life, I swore to God that night that I would never lie again. I would never again try to make myself or my life anything other than what I was, what it was. It was a very rash thing to promise such things at the age of nine, but I didn't realize that then. If you were to ask me if I kept the promise, I would have to admit that I have not—not perfectly. But I can honestly say I have never lied at any time since that night in even the smallest thing without feeling an immediate reproach, without remembering the promise I made.

That night was the first of many times that I felt God's presence and influence in our new home. Everything about the place inspired me and gave me strength. It is hard to describe. Even physically, I felt secure and empowered here. I learned to be a gymnast here, did somersaults in the open fields without spotters or mats. I rode horses. I explored and relished every nook and cranny of the estate grounds. The natural features of the land—the open fields, the rocks and wooded hills behind the estate, even the air and light seemed special here. But while I loved the new place and most everything I met with in the new town—my friends, my new school—there were also continued tensions in our home. The persistent alcoholism of my uncle and aunt was a constant stress, the sense that we were never one family but two dwelling very much apart in one house, and the growing hostility I began to feel toward my aunt and uncle for various reasons made for many tears and hard days. The sense that somehow I was not as loved by my father as my two half-sisters, not as much a part of his life, also started to grow in me at this time. These were painful things. But mostly, it is the good I remember—the beauty, the sense of God's presence in my life, and the sense that every day was new and promising.

For me, God was not in church so much as he was in "the place." He was in my room at night when I went to sleep, in the physical features of my environment, in the air around me. I felt I could breathe him in when I was sad or upset, and he would strengthen me physically. He opened my eyes to the beauties of nature. One morning, in the middle of winter, I set out for the rocks and caves that I often roamed behind the estate on the hill that led up to another old estate where there was a small lake and swans. There had been an ice storm the night before, and everything—trees, rocks, even frail brown leaves that still clung tenaciously to dry branches—was coated with a paper-thin film of ice. The breeze clicked the branches together, and everything sparkled like diamonds in the morning sun. It was the first time something beautiful made me cry.

Church was good, but not in the same way. It was beautiful at St. Barnabas Episcopal Church, and I continued somehow to go even though I was now the only Episcopalian in the house. No one had to prod me. I enjoyed church—the stained glass, the dark, candle-lit interior, the flowers, the music, the sixteenth-century language of the liturgy. I joined the choir. I went to confirmation classes in the eighth grade and received my confirmation on the third Sunday after Easter in 1958. Everyone confirmed received a copy of the *Book of Common Prayer*. I still have mine.

Maybe it was the beauty of the psalms we read in church every Sunday that made me to want to read the Bible, or maybe it was the importance it had to my other grandmother, my Christian Science grandmother. She was my father's mother, the one who had tried so hard to adopt his political radicalism in the '30s and '40s. By the '50s, however, health problems had caused her to abandon politics and look back to her faith. In the years I knew her, her daily routine always included sitting down to Mary Baker Eddy's *Science and Health with a Key to the Scriptures* and the *King James Bible.* She was really the only person I knew who read the Bible. Whenever I visited with her, she would share verses with me and impress on me the importance of reading the Bible for its spiritual truths rather than its literal words. Whatever the cause, sometime in the late '50s, I asked my grandfather to buy me a Bible for my birthday. We shopped for it together and got a beautiful King James Version with black and white etchings on thick, silky paper. I read it as I would have read a novel—straight through—or almost straight through. I think I bogged down around Daniel. Something about the Bible impressed me. I remembering telling a friend, in one of those adolescent kinds of conversations about what one book you would take if you were stranded on a desert island and could only have one book for your whole life, that I would take the Bible, not because I attached such great religious importance to it, but because it had been so important to so many people throughout human history. I felt it had to be pretty rich in content to be popular so long.

The Bible was not the only religion book I read. As I got into high school, I was interested in religion generally and read a number of books having to do with the topic. I had a terrible weakness for sensuous looking (and feeling) books, a weakness I think God used to expose me to books I might otherwise never have touched. It was this that attracted me to a small edition of John Woolman's *Journal*.[1] It was my first contact with Quaker writing and thinking. My father bought it for me on a visit I had with him in the city. I had never heard of Woolman or Quakerism, but the tiny red volume with the silk ribbon bookmark drew my eye and called me to possess it. My father had heard of Woolman's work against slavery and the boycott of slave-made goods he led in the eighteenth century; these were things even a thoughtful atheist could respect. I was very influenced by the book. Woolman's integrity, the simplicity of his Christian faith, the seriousness with which he approached the moral evil of slavery impressed me. It impressed me so much that I got my other grandfather, my father's step-father (married to the Christian Scientist), to take me to a Quaker Meeting in Scarsdale, New York, to see what Quakerism looked like "in the flesh." The Meeting had no decorative features at all—something I am not sure I appreciated just then. People filed in quietly and sat down on pew-like benches that were arranged to face an empty table in the center. There was no stained glass, no minister, no music, no Bible reading, no prayer—only silence, utter silence for a full hour. I cannot now remember if anyone said anything in the hour we were there. We took a few brochures when we left. It interested me, but we didn't go back.[2] The seed, however, was planted. The Quakers would never be wholly out of the picture again.

I sometimes try to imagine what my Marxist father must have thought—watching his daughter become so interested in and drawn to religion, sometimes even as a result of things he had said or introduced me to. He clearly wanted me to go a different way. From the earliest times, I remember talks we had in which he expressed skepticism and curiosity about how I could be drawn to something that seemed so unconvincing and unappealing to him. But he was a very tactful person and very accepting of what I thought, even when I was very young.

In my last two years of high school, I became very interested in other literature as well, through English class and other outside reading. Some of what I was drawn to was also to play a role in the development of my thinking and my faith. One was James Joyce's *Portrait of the Artist as a Young Man*. The whole theme of Stephen's search for a father touched me in a vulnerable place. Joyce did not intend his writing to draw readers to the Catholicism, and little in the book is positive about the Church, but it drew me anyway—the searing identity it impressed on Stephen, the inescapable claim of it over him. I did not respond to it immediately, but I know it played a role in how I felt myself bound to it later on. But by far the most important piece of literature I was exposed to in high school was T. S. Eliot's *Four Quartets*. We read the opening segment of it in English class my senior year:

> Time present and time past
> Are both perhaps present in time future.
> And time future contained in time past.
> If all time is eternally present
> All time is unredeemable.
> What might have been is an abstraction
> Remaining a perpetual possibility
> Only in a world of speculation.
> What might have been and what has been
> Point to one end, which is always present.[3]

It wasn't an easy poem, and poetry wasn't really my "thing" then or ever. I might never have even remembered reading it in high school had I not rediscovered it a few years later in college. But when I did, when it did become important, I remembered it as having come into my life in high school. Grace works in this way, unheralded and almost unperceived in its entries into our lives.

But religion and the pieces that made up religion for me was only one part of the person I was in high school and in later life. Because of the strange shape of my family life, there was a kind of fault line that ran through the landscape that I had to negotiate, a philosophical and emotional fault line that separated the worlds of my parents and grandparents. The fault line ran through me as well—on the one side, the conventional religion and politics my grandparents fostered in me; on the other, the politically and philosophically radical outlooks my parents fostered.

My visits with both my father and my sister were always extended conversations on everything that was going on in the world at that time: developments in science, psychology, and culture, understanding the dynamics of human life and history, the events of the day—civil rights, the cold war, the Cuban Revolution, the presidential campaign of 1960. From them I learned that you couldn't necessarily trust what you saw on the television or read in the daily newspapers. You had to keep in mind the interests your source of information was out to serve, where they got their money, what they were trying to convince their readers of, and where they got their information. And my father and sister tried to get me to see that the government could sometimes do very bad things—like try to murder Fidel Castro or undermine the revolution he had brought to Cuba. They also tried to get me to see that most of the things most people believed most fervently—their religious hopes and patriotic idealism—were things that mostly benefited the rich and powerful but did not necessarily serve the interests of the poor and oppressed. I didn't know until later in my life that my father was a member of the Communist Party—or had been. To this day I am not sure when he was. I know he joined and eventually quit, but not the details. The closest he came to admitting it to me was when I told him that I might someday like to run for Congress and he advised, laughing to himself, that I perhaps should keep my relationship with him a little quiet if I did. But it wasn't the politics of communism we talked about. It was the philosophical underpinnings—the dynamics of history, seeing through conventions, unmasking the illusions bourgeois society generated to hide the ugly economic underbelly of reality.

My mother and sister also did their best to bring me over to that side. The few memories I have of visiting my mother in New York involve not only memories of bubble baths and walks to the park but also tirades against President Eisenhower for the execution of Julius and Ethel Rosenberg, talk of the street demonstrations protesting it, or other angry remarks about the country. My sister was among the first group of American students who went to Cuba after the revolution in 1960. She came back a complete convert, full of enthusiastic stories about the new society Castro was bringing about in Cuba, the hope it represented for all the poor countries of Central and South America, and the challenge it represented to American capitalism and imperialism. She had pictures of the new housing going up for the poor in Cuba, the preschools that were being started, the medical care that was being provided for free. Everything she told me, I believed. I carried copies of my sister's pictures of Cuba to school with me and argued with teachers and others in my classes about what was going on there. My parents and sister seemed so much better informed than anyone else I knew about politics and current events that it was just not possible to disbelieve what they told me. But I didn't let them disturb the other side of my own inner fault line, not yet. My interest and involvement in my church, my love of the Kennedys—these loyalties and loves were in some little compartment of me that was beyond the reach of other people's doubts or criticisms, even my father's. He seemed to accept that. He didn't challenge me seriously on my lack of consistency. I think he understood that I was living in two worlds, that I was learning different things in the different places of my life, and that it would take time for me to resolve the inconsistencies. He believed his views were true, and that if he was patient, I would come around to seeing things his way. And I would, for a while.

My freshman year at college (1963–64) saw the culmination of all the early God-oriented, God-believing parts of my life. The innocent mysticism that had been a part of my life since I was ten became incredibly intense. I thought about God all the time—I felt his presence in the sky at night; I felt his power in the sea and in the many beauties of nature; I felt love present in these things. And I believed that there were logical reasons to believe in God's existence, reasons that had to do with the necessity of having some objective foundation for the moral laws we all seemed to believe existed. I remember even having arguments on the point with my father and feeling surprised that while he did not accept that proposition, he had no really cogent argument to make against it.

But while my mystical experiences grew ever stronger, my loyalty to the Episcopal Church eroded. I started having trouble understanding the legitimacy of the break Henry VIII had made with Rome. Somehow, his desire to get a divorce and marry a woman who could give him an heir didn't seem very convincing to me as the basis of my church's existence. I started to feel the pull of the Catholic Church, the church that traced its origins back to the apostles. I spent hours in the lowest level of the college library stacks—where the religion books were—reading the *Catholic Encyclopedia,* reading Catholic philosophers like Thomas Aquinas, trying to understand, trying to come to some decision about where I should be as a Christian. I argued with committed Catholics about things that bothered me about the Catholic Church, but while I never gave them the satisfaction of knowing it, I eventually began to see things their way. But it wasn't just logic or argument that won me. There were emotional reasons as well. The Catholic Church, after all, had been the church I had attended with my grandmother in my earliest childhood. It had been the church of most of the people in my family, some of whom I haven't mentioned but whom I greatly admired—my mother's younger brother, for example, and his wife. They were devoutly Catholic and were wonderful models of Catholic piety. And the Catholic Church was in the news in 1960 and 1961, with the campaign of John F. Kennedy and the opening by Pope John XXIII of the Second Vatican Council.

But Catholicism was not the only thing I looked at. As fate (or providence) would have it, my freshman year also saw me housed across the hall from a Quaker student who reminded me of the virtues I had found in my brief encounter with Friends—their integrity, simplicity, commitment to social justice, and moral earnestness. I gave some thought to becoming a Friend. I don't remember how much time or effort I gave to exploring Quakerism that year—probably not that much, but I know I talked about it with at least one friend. I remember expressing to her that I found Friends too "spiritual"—too inward—to appeal to me. They didn't *do* things—they didn't kneel or cross themselves, they didn't take communion or do confession, nothing. These outward things were somehow important to me at this time of my life.

The summer after my freshman year, I sought out a priest and received instruction. In August, I was received into the Catholic Church. I remember that the priest thought I might be proceeding a little too quickly, but he knew that my family was mostly Catholic, so it seemed natural to him that I should end up there. For some reason, I was rebaptized and reconfirmed even though I had had these sacraments in the Episcopal Church. I think it was a matter of not really being sure at the time where I had had these things done or not having any proof of them. Then I was confessed and received. I remember thinking even then what a miracle it was that I should ever have chosen to become a Catholic, that I should ever have been granted faith when so few in my family were believers. One of the other wonderful things that happened as a result of my conversion was that my grandfather, who had not been to church in thirty years, took the occasion of my conversion to return to the Church. It was a sign of how he loved me that he did it. I wish I had appreciated it more. To celebrate the great day, I bought myself a lovely red leather-bound missal with gold-edged pages and a bright blue rosary!

My father, of course, did not get it. He did not understand how I could overlook the horrors of the Inquisition or the reactionary role the Catholic Church played (as he saw it) in history and in the societies where Catholicism was established. He didn't find any of my arguments about the moral law or about the sense I had of God's presence in the universe logical or convincing, but it wasn't his way to write me off or give me a hard time. He just shook his head and said he "just didn't get it."

All the parts of the puzzle that life was to be for me, intellectually and spiritually at least, were on the table by the time I was seventeen: the experiences I had of God's reality as a child, my interest in religion generally, a sense of conviction about the historical legitimacy of the Catholic Church, a sense of the importance of Scripture, the T. S. Eliot poem, the pull of Quakerism. On the table too were the pieces of the puzzle I had gotten from my father and sister—the skepticism, the Marxism, the interest in science and psychology, the political radicalism. I would move the pieces of this puzzle around and around in the years ahead, throwing out this piece or that, bringing it back, fitting things together, but the pieces themselves never changed much. They were what I had to work with.

3

No Secure Foothold

For a little more than a year after my conversion to Catholicism, I was very happy, but it wasn't to last. The underlying fault line in my thinking between faith and doubt, mysticism and rationalism, trust and skepticism was just too unstable to build on. I am not even sure how much faith, or what I would now call faith, there was in my conversion. Was it a conversion or was it just a human decision about which church had the best arguments institutionally? I had an intense sense of God's spiritual presence in the universe, an intellectual belief that God's existence was necessary if anything were to be thought "good" or "evil" in human history and human affairs, and a belief that human beings must be free in some sense if moral acts were to have any reality at all. I definitely believed the argument made by Ivan Karamazov in *The Brothers Karamazov* that if God did not exist, then anything could be permitted, but I had no real sense of personally *needing* God in my life, no real sense of sin, and little appreciation for Christ's role in the religion that bore his name. My sense of God was very diffuse and mysterious, very tied up with nature, and my love of the Church had more to do with beautiful *things* like Bibles, missals, and stained glass and with cultural and intellectual traditions than it did with any really informed understanding of my need for salvation or holiness of life or discipline. My faith also isolated me from other people rather than bringing me into relation with them on a deeper plane. I had no one with whom I could share my thoughts about it, and its mysteries tended to bring me away from the society of people.

I think it was this isolation that was my greatest weakness. Sometime in my junior year I broke out of this isolation and developed a strong liking for and connection with a teacher and dormitory supervisor of mine, a young and charismatic English instructor. I visited her home in northern Georgia over Christmas, talked with her at length about her childhood and growing up in the Baptist Church, how debilitating in many ways she felt the fundamentalism of her family's faith had been in her own life, and how dramatically she had rejected it. I probably shared some of my own checkered background and gave her my own sense of what was true, but I don't really remember all I might have said about my own faith. In any case, she stunned me when she suddenly turned to me in the course of some conversation and said, "I don't know how anyone as intelligent as you can be a Roman Catholic." I felt my faith drain out of me as I sat there.

Why this friend's disapproval was so powerful to me when the disapproval of my father and older sister had been ineffective in undermining my faith over the years, I do not understand. I think it had a lot to do with just needing her as a friend, needing friendship and connection with people generally. She made me want to be close to people, real people—not just "mankind." She made me want to experience things I hadn't experienced, dare things I hadn't dared. But it was also true that the faith I had was not very well grounded in me. The rational difficulties with which faith always contends suddenly mushroomed into insurmountable barriers.

The disdain of religion that my friend communicated to me was not a disdain confined to her. It was more and more the voice of the era. My own family had spoken with this voice for years, but by 1965 it could be heard everywhere. It had even been an integral part of my own mental make-up—the skepticism of it, the political and social dimensions of it. For a while it had lived side by side with this other part—this mystical part that saw God everywhere. But now the doubt drove out everything inconsistent with itself. It astonishes me even now to remember how quickly and completely I cast aside all the proofs I had been given of God's reality—the experiences I had had of him, all the interest I had been given in religion, all the joy and nourishment I had drawn from it as a child and young adult.

In the place of faith, I set up ideology. I quickly embraced the political and psychological ideas my sister had been trying to get me to accept over the years. According to these theories, I had been drawn to religion because of the brokenness of my family situation. God was the father I had never had and all the talk of heaven and God's providence was only a form of wishful thinking—projecting human attributes and qualities out onto the universe. Marx and Freud were the ones who could help me make sense of these things—they, along with the intellectuals who built on their insights, were the resources I would turn to in the next years of my life.

The only good thing I can say about the turn away from religion in my life was that it did help me to overcome the isolation I had drifted into. My abandonment of religion was accompanied by immediate efforts on my part to get closer to friends at college. I started to go out at night to small restaurants where students drank beer and smoked. I began smoking and drinking within weeks of losing my faith. I don't mean to say by this that religion itself had been any kind of a bulwark against these vices in me. It hadn't been. It was just that jettisoning religion brought me closer to my peers and these were the things one did with peers in college. Not to partake would have seemed priggish.

The summer between my junior and senior year, which I spent in New York City, also saw the end of my sexual innocence and my introduction into the new world of "hippies," drugs, and generalized rebellion against "the establishment." I spent the summer on the West Side of Greenwich Village in New York. I started going to anti-Vietnam War demonstrations in Washington. I drifted into dreaming about the prospects of revolution, toyed with the idea of organizing a chapter of Students for a Democratic Society on the campus of my college, and just generally got into the late sixties scene.

In my senior year, my disaffection with everything—government, country, and American culture—reached such a pitch that I decided to leave the country forever. I would move to Europe and become an expatriate like Camus—in Paris preferably—be an intellectual, try to find people who understood where history was going and who were interested in making a better future. I made plans to work in a suburb of Paris and purchased tickets to travel one way to Europe by freighter—nothing else seemed apropos. What I would do to make a living, what skills I would bring to the world—none of these things seemed relevant. The world was on the verge of revolution. You couldn't just settle into the system that existed, so you might as well strike out and see what was around, what was going on in more "progressive" places.

Before moving to that stage of my journey, however, it is important to mention one last thing about college. In my last year at college, I rediscovered Eliot's *Four Quartets.* A routine assignment in a modern poetry class was to write a long study of any modern poem. It didn't need to be a research paper, but it had to be a thorough personal analysis. Rather than reading a poem over and over, I decided to take out a recording I could listen to so I could really get a feel for the work. I came across a record of Eliot reading his *Four Quartets*. As soon as I started listening to it, I realized it was the poem I had read in high school. I listened to it over and over until I knew much of it by heart. I fell in love with it in a way I have never loved any piece of literature, but I would stop short of saying I understood it. Like many great poems, it was elusive, but there were parts of it that hit me hard. It seemed to capture in a poetic way many of the mysteries I had found so alluring in religion—that sense of a reality that reached beyond time; the oneness we felt with human beings who had come before us in time or who would come after us; the irrepressible intuition we had that there was some ultimate significance to human existence. Over the next fifteen years, the poem would keep alive in me a small place where faith continued to be valid.

In May of 1967, I graduated, packed everything I owned into a big trunk, and headed for Europe. I went to Hampton Roads, Virginia, where the freighter waited that would take me there. It was a German freighter, carrying coal and twenty to thirty passengers as well. A coal freighter may not sound like an appealing conveyance, but once the anchor was struck and the coal dust was washed away, it was every bit as wonderful as a cruise ship. In fact, I doubt a cruise ship could have been as enjoyable. As luck would have it—having never traveled by freighter—I arrived at the dock several days before the passengers were supposed to arrive. With annoyance, the crew brought me and my trunk on board a day early and tried to make me feel welcome. The captain, a handsome German, took me under his wing and introduced me to everyone on board. There were two other officers, one German and one Dutch, the wife of the German second mate, who was traveling with him, and a Turkish radio operator, who was both the first Muslim and one of the loveliest men I ever met.

It was a magical ten days. We enjoyed warm weather, calm seas, and all the comforts of first-class travel—delicious food, good company, and a small swimming pool filled with the beautiful, blue Gulf Stream waters we were traveling through. I shared a spacious cabin with another young American woman, a co-ed from Montana. The window in our room was so large that I could sit beside it for hours and gaze out at the endlessly variable waves and crystal clear skies until I was intoxicated with their beauty. At night I joined with the crew and the German woman on board for games and dancing and talk. I practiced my German, and they practiced their English. I had taken German for only year in college, so I didn't know much. The experience I had on board the ship shifted my sights with respect to Europe. While I had previously known no one and was heading for a very theoretical place, now I knew real people from somewhere in Europe. Paris suddenly didn't seem so exclusively irresistible to me by the time I landed. After spending a few days in Paris and only one night in the house where I had been employed as an *au pair,* I changed my plans. I left all my worldly possessions, asking my *au pair* family to please turn my trunk over to the French Salvation Army, and headed out for northern Germany, where the people I had met on the ship lived. I visited with the woman I had met and found a summer job with a wealthy Hamburg family babysitting their three small children. This family then helped me find a better job teaching English at a girls' school outside of Hamburg.

The year of my exile was not terribly eventful. I attended some impressive antiwar demonstrations in Berlin and got to know a radical or two. Radicalism in Europe was much more politically sophisticated than in America, more ideological and hopeful of success than anything I had known in the States. It was a turbulent year in Europe, but my limited ability to communicate with people, along with my foreignness, made it impossible for me to feel part of things. In June of 1968, therefore, I returned to the United States. The summer I returned was as turbulent in the U.S. as it had been in Europe—a time of assassinations and street riots, a time of radical organizing and presidential campaigns, teachers' strikes and racial unrest. It was a terrible time really. For a few months, I stayed with my sister in New York City. She was a teacher there at the time, involved in a bitter school decentralization struggle that had resulted in a lengthy teachers' strike. I worked for a few months as an assistant editor at a financial magazine there, but soon moved on to graduate school. I had been admitted to the graduate school at the University of North Carolina at Chapel Hill. I left early with the thought of establishing residence there for the six months required to call myself an in-state student.

There was turmoil there too—striking cafeteria workers and radicalized students. But as radicalized as people seemed, there was a hedonistic element to the movement in this country I had not seen in Europe. Things were not so much political here as they were just culturally tumultuous. Drugs were prevalent, Woodstock fever captured people, a sense of pessimism about the prospects for change pervaded the streets. I settled into life as a graduate student and got caught right up in the atmosphere and events of the day. I joined the daily protests in town against the university's treatment of its cafeteria workers. I attended meetings where women complained about the difficulties of being taken seriously even in the radical organizations that had sprung up. I got myself a job and a place to stay. I tried to start studying some things that had interested me in Europe—German literature and music. But mostly the social aspects of life predominated. Men were easy to meet. I flitted from one to the other for a while with little thought or emotion. I fell in love one time and suffered rejection. I dabbled a little in drugs when other people offered them, but did not see the allure. And I got swept up in the frenzy of demonstrations that came in the wake of the Cambodian invasion and the Kent State killings. We shut the university down. Exams were postponed or cancelled. People went to Washington to join huge demonstrations, but there was no clear leadership or plan for any real change. It was all very politically superficial.

Religion got very little thought at this point in my life, but there is one small detail I probably should mention. Just after arriving in Chapel Hill, on my first tour of the campus and student bookstore, I bought a Bible. The Bible I had had in high school had been among the things abandoned in Paris when I left to go to Germany. The new one, a *Jerusalem Bible* newly translated from the French, was nice too, leather bound with gilt edges. The beauty of the book was probably what drew me to it. Mostly, however, it was studies and men that filled my life and left little time for anything else.

Sometime during the fall of 1969, just after the one painful romance I have mentioned, I met man up the street from where I lived who was different from the others. He wasn't into "the Chapel Hill scene" or politics. He had dropped out of high school to join the Marines and then left the Marines to go home to a dying father. He was now finishing up his studies for his bachelor's degree. He was a nice, decent man, and we soon took to each other. I liked him—not like the man I had been disappointed by, but he seemed better than that man. By the time I began thinking about what my relationship with him was to be, my way of thinking such things through had become psychologically complicated in a way that would prove disastrous. It wasn't that I wanted to be calculating or dishonest. It's just that I started from the premise that my inner judgment about things was not to be trusted. My whole emotional make-up seemed geared to mislead and disappoint me. I attributed it to my childhood. I picked men to love whom I subconsciously knew would reject me because that was the pattern I had experienced with my father. My instincts were faulty. I needed somehow to work around them. The fact that all of this was unmitigated nonsense did not seem obvious to me at the time. I had been raised by a man—my grandfather—who had been utterly devoted to me and self-sacrificing. My father, while I had not lived with him, had also been attentive and supportive. But these realities did not support the sense I had of myself as abused and rejected and needy. So I convinced myself that if I wanted to find someone who would treat me right, I had to discount my "gut" feelings and go with my head. That is exactly what I did. I liked this man, but I didn't love him. We had little in common, but I did feel I could trust him. It never occurred to me to wonder if I could be trusted to be loving and faithful to him over time.

In June of 1970, some six or seven months after I met this man, we were married. I finished up my course work for my Master's in English and we moved to Winston-Salem, where my husband had found a job and I planned to enroll in classes I needed to become certified to teach. By September, I knew I had made a terrible mistake. We were too entirely different, and there were things about him and about his temperament I found troubling, most of which I will not go into here. It would not be fair. But I stayed. I continued to distrust my inner sense of things. We moved around from place to place, a pattern that would prove constant. In the first year, we moved from Winston-Salem to Florida, from Florida to Raleigh, and from Raleigh to Boone, North Carolina. In Boone, I got pregnant. We went back to Raleigh. The logistics of moving from place to place made finding decent work impossible. I took a correspondence course and became certified to teach English, then took the law boards and thought of going to law school.

Marriage took my mind off of politics to some extent, but it's clear when I reflect on these years that I still saw myself as very much the radical. In Winston-Salem I made contact with the Black Panther Party, had a long conversation with one of their leaders about the need for revolutionary change, donated a typewriter, and even rented a car for them a time or two. When we returned to Raleigh and I was pregnant, I worked on the McGovern Campaign. It was there I made the acquaintance of the next Quaker who would influence me. I told her of my old interest in Friends, and she told me I should try to come to Meeting sometime, but I didn't feel led. By the time our baby—a son—was born, my husband and I had decided that I should go to law school. Becoming a lawyer would take the economic pressure off of him and give the family a degree of security—at least that was the thought. How being a lawyer would fit with my own need to be a mother to my son or other children that might come along was something to which we gave little thought.

I started classes at the law school in Chapel Hill in 1973 when my son was ten months old, but law school only brought more stresses. I started feeling an intense dissatisfaction with the relationship I was in and a strong desire to leave. I also came down with a terrible case of hives undoubtedly related to stress. Sometime that first year, I broached the idea of separating, but my husband told me bluntly that if I even thought of leaving, he would take the baby and disappear forever. I backed off. I tried to resign myself to the situation. I thought of all the billions of women in history who had lived their lives with men they hadn't chosen or men with whom they hadn't been happy, and I resigned myself to the fact that I would be one of them.

The hives tormented me. They came every night, all over my body, itching and swelling as they blossomed. In the morning they started to recede, so that by late morning only smooth reddish blotches remained. They would be gone by afternoon. At night it would start again—every night, every day for a year. I tried to take medication, but the narcotic effect made studying and driving to school impossible. I tried hypnotism, but I couldn't be hypnotized. One doctor tried a kind of guided meditation that he said had worked with other people. He had me close my eyes and imagine myself in a comfortable, nice place, someplace I had really been, someplace I loved. The place I thought of was the shore at Ocean Isle, North Carolina, where we went during the summers. He asked me to imagine myself walking there, going somewhere where it was very quiet and peaceful. He asked me where it was. It was the beach. He led me along, asking me to describe the place, to feel myself there, to feel the sun and hear the water breaking on the shore, to feel the warmth of the sand, the warmth of the sun above me. Then he suggested I imagine someone coming down the beach toward me, someone I felt comfortable with, someone who loved me. He suggested I imagine the face coming closer and closer, recognizing me, reacting to my approach. He asked me to concentrate on the person's face. Then he asked me who it was. It was Jesus, I told him.

The exercise did not cure my hives, but it let me know I was still suffering a bad case of religious nostalgia. The hives finally did go as I started my second year in law school, but that year brought challenges of its own. I had a second pregnancy and a miscarriage, then the next spring another pregnancy. By the winter of 1976, I was finished with law school and ready to have my second child. My little boy was three. That Christmas I took him to see the Raleigh Boys Choir. He was old enough now to appreciate Christmas and some of the things I had loved in it. As soon as the choir started to sing, I started to weep uncontrollably. I hid it from my son, I think, and from the people around me, but I again I felt a sense of torment. That Christmas I also took him to the Moravian Church down the street from our home to see the Christmas display and buy Christmas cookies. They had a beautiful crèche scene—a diorama of the Bethlehem countryside, the star, the shepherds, the kings coming over the hills bearing gifts, the stable, the holy family. I didn't expect my son to ask me questions about it, but he did. Suddenly I started giving explanations that would have made a graduate student's head spin—about how some people believed this, but other people believed that, how what was laid out here wasn't really true, but it was what people believed in and what they celebrated at Christmas. He settled for all my words, but I wasn't satisfied. I left there feeling troubled. I wondered how it would be for him and for the other child I was soon to have to grow up without any way of connecting to these simple traditions, without any sense of things "spiritual." My husband did not share these concerns. He did not feel any attraction to religion at all and only spoke angrily of it when he did think about it. But I can't say that I know what his heart might have been on these issues. We simply didn't talk about it. We didn't talk about anything deep very much. Religion had never been a part of our relationship. The nostalgia I felt and the memories I had were things we didn't share. I tended to think of it mostly as bad stuff in me—psychological neediness, irrationality, unhealthy wishful thinking.

In February, my second child, a little girl, was born. Shortly after, I called the Quaker woman I had met and found out where Friends met in town. I needed to bring some kind of spiritual something into my life. I didn't really believe in all the doctrinal paraphernalia religion involved, but Friends did not have any of that. I wanted my children to have a spiritual community to be part of as well, and Friends seemed to fit this bill. So I started to go.

Raleigh Friends had no formal Meeting House. They met in an old, refurbished house near downtown Raleigh. The ten or fifteen people who attended Meeting there simply sat in chairs in a circle in what had once been the living room of this house. On the walls there were a few posters that proclaimed Friends' faith in "that of God" in every man and in the power of peace and kindness; other than that, there was no "religious" message proclaimed here. My friend had told me that Friends, while Christian in their beginnings, were not strictly Christian any more, that people believed all kinds of things. The one common thing, however, was belief in an indwelling Spirit that people looked to. People did not sing in Meeting or pray. Now and then someone would feel "moved to speak," to share a thought or concern, but it was a quiet Meeting. I liked that it was quiet. I brought the children with me—sat my son on my lap and put my infant daughter on a blanket on the floor next to me. They were the only children there most of the time. There was no organized child care, no "First Day School" as they call it. After ten or fifteen minutes of silence, I would take the children out, go upstairs with them where they could play with a few toys and have a snack. People were good about offering to take the children out and watch them so I could experience the Meeting, but more often than not I took them out myself. I remember thinking how silly it was for me to come and then be the one to take them out to give them a "Sunday school" experience—me, who had not the first notion of what to say to them about religion. But I liked the little bit of Meeting I was able to experience. I appreciated the peace and stillness in a way I hadn't expected, and I respected the people there.

Meanwhile, I also prepared to open a law office in downtown Raleigh. I passed the bar exam the summer after my daughter was born and found an office to share. Though I had little time for politics now, my vision of myself as a radical had not changed. I sought out some radical labor organizers in a Greensboro textile mill and told them I would be happy to offer them legal services were they ever needed.

For two years, I attended Quaker Meeting in Raleigh, enjoying the silence and the people who went. I shared the group's social concerns for peace, equality, and justice, and my husband didn't mind my going or taking the children. He shared the concerns for justice that Quakers had, he just felt no desire to go to Meeting. He started having a recurrence of the kind of work panic he had struggled with earlier. At some point not long after I opened my office, he quit his job and left for Washington D.C., jumping at an opportunity there. I am not sure I remember even talking about it with him. Once he was there, however, we talked about moving, and I remember at least one visit the children and I made where we looked at houses and talked about where we might live, but I don't completely remember the timing on the moves and problems we started to have or how these things corresponded to what was going on with me in Meeting. Our marital relationship was beginning to unravel, and the work moves and discontinuities were evidence of the underlying fissure between us.

In Meeting, something peculiar started to happen. I noticed that every time I went and sat down in the silence, my mind would drift to the words of the Eliot poem. It wasn't surprising, I suppose, seeing how much in the poem had to do with stillness:

> At the still point of the turning world. Neither flesh nor fleshless;
> Neither from nor towards; at the still point, there the dance is,
> But neither arrest nor movement. And do not call it fixity,
> Where past and future are gathered.[1]

Or

> Words move, music moves
> Only in time; but that which is only living
> Can only die. Words, after speech, reach
> Into the silence. Only by the form, the pattern,
> Can words or music reach
> The stillness, as a Chinese jar still
> Moves perpetually in its stillness.[2]

In a way, the Meeting was a kind of embodiment of the poem, a place where the "intersection of the timeless with time" was palpable. I couldn't call what I encountered here God yet, but I could call it "that of God," as Quakers suggested. I didn't understand it—that sense of something transcendent that plagued my mind. I didn't feel comfortable with it. But I could not deny that it was something constant in my make-up or experience. The words evoking it began to seem like an obsession. Every time I came into Meeting, I could think of nothing else. It occurred to me at some point that this sense of preoccupation and agitation was what Friends meant by feeling moved to speak, but I didn't feel ready. I didn't have anything to say about the words, no erudite observations or points to make about them as people sometimes did with things they had read. But finally after a year or so I just began to feel that I had to say the words to be rid of them. As I prepared to do it, my heart started to pound. In seconds it was pounding so hard I thought the palpitations must be visible. I looked around to see if anyone was staring at me, noticing my blouse move, but no. It crossed my mind that perhaps it was nerves, that I was anxious because I was going to stand up and speak in front of others, but that was silly. I knew everyone in Meeting well, and I wasn't a shy person about speaking. I was a lawyer, for heaven's sake. At last I spoke. I probably said the lines I have mentioned here, or others like them—lines that spoke of past and future being together in time present or spoke of the intersection of the timeless with time or about time being unredeemable and always present. I don't know. But once the words passed my lips, they were gone. It was the only time I spoke in this Meeting. I didn't connect the call to speak in any clear way with God or even "that of God," I just thought of it as a psychological phenomenon—obsessive thoughts given release. Later I would realize and acknowledge that God had come to me in those words, that he had given me an experience of his presence and of "vocal ministry" as Quakers practice it, but I wasn't yet ready to see it.

My family situation continued to become more and more difficult. No sooner did we seem to set on a plan than some deeper confusion would overtake us. If I seem to have been passive in the face of the moves my husband made at this time, it is because I had no real desire to practice the law I had been prepared to practice. I had two small children and my greatest desire was to be with them. If a move to Washington would permit this, I was for it. But my husband made no provision for us to move there. Then he suddenly changed jobs again and moved back to North Carolina—to Asheville, a small city in the mountains. By this time it was the winter of 1978. Sometime in January, circumstances forced our hand. We had a terrible storm in Raleigh, and a tree fell on our frail little cottage. The roof was badly damaged. It became necessary to leave and join my husband in Asheville, even though he had no proper place to live. He was rooming with his supervisor while he looked for housing. Suddenly we were there, all of us sleeping on the floor of his supervisor's spare bedroom. I found a job working for a federally funded health care organization, using my legal training to help them see to it that they were in compliance with federal health care regulations. In a month or so, we found a house to buy, but things were not good.

I was depressed. My sense of myself at the time was that I had suffered a great deal of unhappiness in life. I had come from a broken family and been separated from a father I had loved deeply. I had had a number of devastating relationships that had left me feeling unloved and unlovable and had stumbled into a bad marriage and tried hard to make it work under very trying circumstances. I had no desire to hurt the man I had married so thoughtlessly, no desire to inflict on my children the kinds of heartaches I had grown up with, but my sense of resilience was gone. I wondered if there might not be some limit to the unhappiness I could endure. My mother had gone crazy in her late thirties. My sister had been in therapy for twenty years and still did not seem entirely well to me. I didn't come from good mental stock. I felt vulnerable and anxious. People didn't know very much about schizophrenia. Some thought it was inherited, some thought it was environmentally induced. I felt that either way I had reason to worry. I had tried to see my situation in a larger way—as something that united me with women throughout history. I had tried to resign myself to living with my mistake. I had tried to throw myself into my work and my children and ignore the things I was powerless to change, but nothing I tried lifted the darkness I saw ahead if I stayed. I told my husband I wanted to separate.

The year that followed was the worst year of my life. It took several months after I told him for us to actually separate. Sometime in the fall of 1978, he moved out of the house. Indeed, he moved out of the state. A month or so after he moved out, he came and took our eight-year-old son out of school and headed for Canada with him. My husband had been born in Canada and held Canadian citizenship, but he did not reckon with Canadian border police who, when he said he was moving back, asked him to show proof of custody for his son. In despair, he turned around and brought him home after forty-eight horrible hours. Thinking that this had been an isolated act of despair, I foolishly neglected to mention the abduction attempt to the judge when our case came up for hearing on the matter of custody in the spring of 1979. The judge ruled that we should have joint custody, with the children having their primary residence with me. Because he was out of the state, though, it meant that he would only get to see them summers and occasional holidays.

A few months later I sent the children down to Georgia, where their father now lived. In July, after having them for several weeks, he returned with our daughter and asked to take our son camping for another few days. I agreed. They didn't come back. The whole time between the first abduction and that summer, he had worked to meet the legal requirements the Canadian border guards would expect from him. He obtained Canadian citizenship papers for our son. He had secured the joint custody decree. I didn't know right away that they had gone to Canada. I wouldn't know that for sure until I found them four months later. I got a letter and tape from them postmarked Hawaii. I hired detectives and tried to pursue the Hawaii lead. Weeks passed. Nothing. Really it is impossible to describe the stress and desperation I felt not knowing where my son was. I feared I would never see him again. I feared the impact it would have on him. I wondered if his father would change his name. I feared for my daughter and wondered how she would deal with the fact that she had been left behind. My sister came down from New York to be with me, to support me and help me think things through. We went down to Georgia to search the rooms my husband had rented there. We found the applications for Canadian citizenship for the children, then we came home. I went to the library and found a book that listed every school district in Canada and I started to write each one. I learned the meaning of finitude. However many districts there were, I would contact them all. I would find my son. It would just take time.

Sometime in the midst of this horror, I headed back to Quaker Meeting, and it was there God found me ready to receive him. I hadn't gone immediately to Quaker Meeting on moving up to Asheville. While I had liked the Meeting in Raleigh, it really hadn't solved the problem I had gone there to solve, the problem of providing my children with some kind of spiritual community and formation. There had been no children's program, and I certainly wasn't capable of providing any structured approach to spiritual matters, so I tried the Unitarian Universalist Church in Asheville and liked it. There was a large and lively congregation there. The minister gave great sermons. The music was upbeat and wonderful and there was a well-attended children's religious education program—not Christian really, but focused on good, positive human values. But now, in the press of despair that closed in on me, positive human values and upbeat music were not what I needed.

4

God Finds Me

I needed something different. I needed the quiet and intimate sense of support and comfort I knew I would find among Friends. I needed to be able to pour my heart out and ask people to "hold me in the light." I needed to reflect on what I had done to get myself into such a mess and ponder ways of getting out of it. Meeting gave me opportunities to do all these things. At some point after starting back, a man came up to me after Meeting and introduced himself to me. This man, who three years later would become my second husband, would become for me in this moment of my life an instrument of God's grace. I didn't realize it at first. We talked about the situation I was in—what I was doing to look for my son, what the status of the search was, how I was holding up. He told me that he was also going through domestic turmoil. His wife had left him and was living somewhere in town. I suppose he shared some sympathetic words, but I cannot remember them now. He also said he was finding comfort reading the Scriptures for the first time, looking to God in a way he had not been willing to do earlier in his life. He was excited about the prophets. They "spoke to his condition," as Friends said.

I started to go to the weekly Bible study he had at his place—an old Victorian house he shared with several other people. We got to know each other. We walked around his neighborhood or mine, talking about our problems, sharing our thoughts about religion. He had been raised a Catholic but had left the Catholic Church in college. He hadn't lost faith entirely though. He continued to feel the pull of the divine, just not in terms of organized religion. Like many in the late sixties and early seventies, he found a degree of spiritual satisfaction in the back-to-nature movement that was big on American college campuses in those years. His hero was Henry David Thoreau. In the years since college, however, with his marriage and entry into the world of private school teaching, he had struggled with depression and felt the need to reattach himself to a spiritual community of some kind. Through a Quaker friend of his wife's, he became interested in Friends and started attending a Meeting near the school where he was teaching. As with many people attracted to Friends during this period, the traditional Friends commitment to things like social justice, peace, and environmental responsibility weighed heavily with him, but he also loved the unadorned Christianity he met with there. Unfortunately, the turn toward religion on his part became yet another tension in his marriage. By the time he and his wife came to Asheville in 1974, their marriage was in trouble. There were no children, but he regretted deeply the failure of the marriage, even more as he found himself drawn to God. He was sure God *could* heal the breach between him and his wife if they would only permit it, but his wife was not a person of faith, and he did not know how it all would end. The only thing he felt sure about was the need to give the matter time and remain open to God's will.

I was in a completely different place with respect to both religion and my marital troubles. I was pretty much a mess, spiritually and psychologically. I had no sense of where I was going religiously at all. For years I had wrestled with feelings of nostalgia for the Church and what it represented to me, but my mind could not seem to find a way back. It wasn't enough to yearn for faith or have an amorphous sense of a transcendent dimension to human life. These I could easily attribute to my psychological neediness. I was morbidly preoccupied with the state of my mind. I had separated, in part, out of a fear that my mind would not hold up over time to the unhappiness I experienced in that union, and what I was going through now made me even more afraid. The abduction of my son was devastating.

I wondered daily how long I could endure it. I kept thinking of something I had read about Virginia Woolf and her descent into mental illness, about how it was like sensing sharks in the waters around her mind—the fear of its inevitability, the inner awareness that the attack was coming and that she was powerless to defend against it. I wanted to believe—now more than ever—but I just couldn't. I was willing to concede that something "spiritual," something we could not know distinctly but called God, might exist; but the whole Christian thing—the man Jesus, the miracles, his dying for our sins, the resurrection, the gospel, the church, the whole array of doctrines and moral mandates—all of this was simply beyond me.

I particularly remember one conversation my friend and I had about Jesus when he asked me what I thought about Jesus' crucifixion. I said I couldn't understand making so much of this one death, terrible as it was, that thousands of men had been crucified by the Romans and that people died all the time for love of others or for causes they thought worthy or good. There was nothing in that story that compelled me intellectually. It would be nice to be able to believe in it, but I couldn't.

How this changed over the weeks and months ahead, I cannot really explain except to call it grace. To the extent I can analyze it, it involved a number of things. The first was my miserable condition and the vulnerability it created in me. It cannot be an accident that I, like so many others, found God in the midst of profound personal suffering. But it was not only my condition. It was also this new relationship and the faith perspective my friend brought to it. He understood a good deal of what I was only just getting ready to receive, and he was able to help me see it with a clarity I most certainly would not have been capable of on my own. But I think the most important element in the mix was the perspective early Quaker thinkers (theologians in the sense that their thoughts were all about God) brought to the Christian gospel. My friend introduced me to these writers and mediated their ideas to me in a way I would not have been able to do on my own.

The relationship developing between us was the cauldron in which everything came together. As with so many people in our situation—in the terminal stages of marital turmoil, miserable and lonely and facing the future with a sense of great failure and emptiness—there was a powerful temptation for both of us to race immediately into a new relationship. I had lived for years in a marriage without feeling much love for or companionship with the man I had married. Now here was a man who was different. He was more like me in background and education, more interested in the things I was interested in, and he bore none of the debris that burdened my old relationship. He was great with children. He had always wanted them and was wonderful with my three-year-old daughter. And for him too, I represented a new face—someone he could talk to about his religious longings and not feel the old barriers and conflicts he had had with his wife. So we gravitated toward each other, and the strong feelings we developed for each other—sexual and otherwise—were soon something we had to deal with.

In these days—the sixties and seventies—sex was not one of those things that young people linked with morality or immorality as we understood it. Morality had to do with social wrongs—violence, exploitation, dishonesty, or lack of respect for others. Sex, as long as it was mutually desired and "not hurtful" was just not in this category. Indeed, if you felt inhibitions with respect to nonexploitative sex, you were considered unhealthy or repressed, a hapless victim of our Puritan or Victorian heritage. But we were not hung-up by these things. We were both separated. I had been separated for nearly a year at this point and was preparing to file for divorce. He had been abandoned by his wife; she had left him months ago and was pursuing her own new relationships.

But something else was in the picture now. My friend was in rebellion against this "sixties mentality." He was beginning to question the "wisdom" our generation was trumpeting to the world. He was seeking something more reliable, more tested. He was beginning to feel the weight of God's presence in his life and was interested in what God's will was for him. Just because you had a strong desire for something didn't necessarily make it "right"—something pleasing to God and beneficial to your deepest nature. He wanted to build on sturdier ground than he had built on previously, and his encounter with Quakerism had helped orient him in his struggle. He was concerned with things I had never heard of or thought about—things like prophetic obedience and the need to test his "leadings" (his personal insights and feelings) against the tradition and the Scriptures. He didn't "feel free" to walk away from his marriage yet, to do anything that might create a barrier to healing the relationship, even though it appeared to be over. He wanted to do what God wanted him to do, and he wanted to do it in God's time. That meant waiting for "clearness." It meant waiting to discern what God wanted him to do. This was his principal concern; it was this concern that had led him back to the early writings of Friends and to the Bible for guidance. I've mentioned that he was reading the prophets. The passage I remember him speaking of most often was from Jeremiah:

> Thus says the Lord:
> Stand at the crossroads, and look,
> and ask for the ancient paths,
> where the good way lies; and walk in it,
> and find rest for your souls (Jer. 6:16).

This was what he wanted to do—find his way back to the "ancient paths," walk in them, and find his peace there. We talked a lot about the prophets and our generation's rejection of the "ancient paths," our efforts to forge a new way of defining "the good way," a way rooted not in religious tradition but in subjective, personal judgments about what was right and wrong. How could you find your way back to these paths? Early Quakers said that "Christ's light" was the light that illumined the way, and Christ was telling him that he was just "not free" right now to do what he wanted. I didn't understand it entirely, but I did understand that I had to be patient, that I couldn't hope for things to work out with him unless he felt inwardly ready to move on. The thing we wanted, the freedom we sought, had to be given—not seized.

It is not surprising that one of the first things I shared with him was the poem I had loved for so many years. It seemed to speak to our condition too. I must have shared it with him because he wrote to me thanking me for introducing him to these words:

> I said to my soul, be still, and wait without hope
> For hope would be hope for the wrong thing; wait without love
> For love would be love of the wrong thing; there is yet faith
> But the faith and the love and the hope are all in the waiting.[1]

This was what we had to do, because this was exactly the situation we were in. We didn't know what it was we should be hoping for or waiting for. We had to be patient; we had to lay down our wills, or at least try to. Early Quakers had written a lot on the subject of patience:

> . . . stand still in quietness and meekness, that the still voice you may hear, which till you come down within, you cannot hear. . . . So be low and still, if you will hear his voice. . . . This gift is free, and offered freely to all who will receive it; and yet you cannot receive the gift in your own wills, but through the denial of your own will. For the light is contrary to the will. . . . As you receive the will of God, you deny your own wills. . . .[2]

So we struggled with feelings we could not avoid yet somehow felt we had to set aside if we ever wanted to feel the kind of inner clarity and rightness these passages point to. My friend reminded me that the central message of Christ's life was that crucifixion was not the real end of faithfulness—resurrection was. He encouraged me to see the self-denial we were engaged in as a kind of cross we had been given to bear, a crucifixion of our wills and desires that we had to endure if we wanted to come to any kind of real resurrection in our lives, a resurrection that was life not seized but bestowed. Friends had taught him that. The impatient and willful self, what Friends simply called "the flesh," had to be restrained:

> [. . .] that which could not abide in the patience nor endure the fire, in the Light I found to be the groans of the flesh (that could not give up to the will of God), which had veiled me, and that could not be patient in all trials, troubles and anguishes and perplexities, and could not give up self to die by the Cross, the power of God, that the living and quickened might follow him; [. . .][3]

Somewhere in the midst of everything we were going through—the breakup of our marriages, the abduction of my son, the neediness and desire we felt in wanting to grab on to one another, I began to see something. It had never occurred to me to think of Christ's crucifixion as something I could connect with in this way. Could it be that this was the way in which it was true—or at least *a* way? My friend thought it was. Early

Friends had seen it that way. I tried to take this view of it. Even if things never worked out for us in a worldly or fleshly way, the death of that impatience in us would surely lead to some good, some kind of resurrected life that would be better than anything we could fashion in our own wills.

I don't remember exactly how it started to change, but suddenly I began to see that this was a way of seeing the cross, a way that illuminated what we were going through day to day, what we were hoping for and waiting for. I was familiar with Christian language and teachings, but I had never heard of Christ spoken of in these terms. He had always been presented as an outward thing to me, a person crucified for sins long ago, or off in heaven somewhere at the right hand of God, wherever that was, or present in the Eucharist or in some other thing or place that was always outside of me. But Friends said Christ was in me. His crucifixion was something to be joined with in the depths of my being. What he was doing in *my* life now was what he had come to do in history, and he was inviting me to be joined to him, to trust as he did in his Father to bring forth something good in his own time. It was startling to me to think of Christ as something present in me. Later, when I came to study what early Friends had taught, it was apparent that they had been startled at the thought too. The following is Isaac Penington's account of his own "convincement":[4]

> The Lord caused his holy power to fall upon me, and gave me such an inward demonstration and feeling of the seed of life, that I cried out in my spirit, *This is he, this is he, there is not another, there never was another. He was always near me though I knew him not,* not so sensibly, not so distinctly, as now he was revealed in me, and to me by the Father.[5]

I had experienced the nearness of God many times in my life: helping me overcome a tangle of lies so I could start life fresh in a new place, comforting me when I felt rejected or strange living apart from my parents, strengthening me when I was afraid of going to sleep, speaking to me out of the night sky when I needed my grandfather not to die, whispering to me in the words of a great poem. *He was always near me though I knew him not, not so sensibly, not so distinctly, as now he was revealed in me . . .*

On the simplest level, what I came to see and then to experience as I let my defenses down and opened myself to the possibility that God and Christ might be real and present to me in this interior kind of way were the two fundamental things early Friends taught: that the Christ of history, the Christ who suffered crucifixion and rose again—the light and word of God that John spoke of in his gospel—dwelled really and palpably in the depths of every human person, and that this Christ was not in us to merely be a presence or aura of some kind, but was a power working in us to redeem us from the spiritual death that is the "normal" or "natural" state of our existence in this world. Christ dwells within you, and he is there to lead you to life.

This was the Quaker message—the early Quaker message. It wasn't a message they invented, but it was one they were clearer about than any other Christians I had ever come in contact with. The Scriptures told us of this Christ. In his second letter to the Corinthian church, Paul writes these words: "Examine yourselves to see whether you are living in the faith. Test yourselves. Do you not realize that Jesus Christ is in you?" (13:5). And John—John knew this Christ:

> He [John the Baptist] . . . was not the light, but he came to testify to the light. The true light, which enlightens everyone, was coming into the world (John 1:8–9).

God's light enlightens every person according to John, and this light came into the world in the person of Jesus. "Abide in me as I abide in you," Christ says to his disciples (John 15:4). The indwelling Christ was the "light" in us that permitted us *to see* God and Christ (see 1 Cor. 2:10–12), to hear God's voice and feel the encouragement of God's love: "All who obey his commandments abide in him, and he abides in them. And by this we know that he abides in us, by the Spirit that he has given us"(1 John 3:24).

These are all familiar passages to people who read the Bible or attend church with any regularity. I had heard and read these passages earlier in my life too, but I had never realized that they meant what they said in any kind of practical way—poetical flourishes or mystical sentiments maybe, but nothing I could relate to my day-to-day life. No one I had ever met as a practicing Episcopalian or Catholic had ever spoken of these things in a way that related them to my experience. But it stood to reason that if Christ's Spirit is really in the human spirit, it must be something you can experience and be in contact with. How does one sense that presence? How does one discern it from all the other things that are present in the human mind and heart? How does it connect with the gospel the apostles preached or the church they established? These were the things Friends spoke of in their preaching and writing. These were the things they focused on in their worship and in the living of their lives.

They talked about "motions" that drew them to God and made them feel his presence and "openings" that helped them comprehend his will. They experienced "pressings" that revealed to them God's displeasure with things that they said or did, and "callings" from him to challenge worldly customs or preach his gospel to the world. These were the things Friends wrote about. I knew what it was to have such "motions," "pressings," and "openings." I had had them one way or another all my life. I had just not been able to see them in the context of the Christ spoken of in Scripture. A few of the "openings" I had had over the course of my life had even survived my atheism. I still believed there was order and design in the universe, and I still felt there was something in human nature that tapped into some transcendent something somewhere.

Now I began to open myself to the idea that it was not just weakness or neediness in me that was at the root of these experiences and intuitions, but something real and necessary and solid—even God himself:

> . . . this is he whom I have waited for and sought after from my childhood, who was always near me, and had often begotten life in my heart, but I knew him not distinctly, nor how to receive him or dwell with him.[6]

I had tried to convince myself that he had been an illusion, but now I could see that he simply needed to be accepted in faith. Friends' way of applying the Christ event to my interior life permitted me to see a validity in it that was so helpful and so powerful spiritually that the intellectual difficulties I had had seemed to pale by comparison. A profound and powerful sense of meaning came from accepting it. Again there were words in the Eliot poem that seemed perfectly to capture what was happening:

> [I had] had the experience but missed the meaning,
> And approach to the meaning restores the experience
> In a different form, beyond any meaning
> We can assign to happiness.[7]

I had had the knowledge of Christ but had missed the connection, and now that I was seeing the connection and the relevance, the knowledge seemed much more credible. How could I have been so willing to set aside these experiences and memories? How could I have turned my back on the life he had begotten in my heart? Early Friends addressed such questions too, and the answers they gave seemed right to me. There was also "that in us" that did not want to respond to God, a part of us that was much more comfortable with the answers the world gave. Francis Howgill, one of the early Friends I liked the best, wrote of this with insight as well:

> It [Christ's word in you] has often checked and called, but you have not answered its call, and so have chosen your own way, and so have gone from the way, which is the light of Christ in you. And so you run into the broad way; and that which desired after God hath not been nourished and fed, but hath been famished and another hath been fed, which now is for the slaughter. But now as you return home to within, to the true Light of Jesus, which is that one thing, which leads all men that own it, and to be guided by it, you shall have true rest and peace.[8]

This was true. I too had famished the part of me that had desired after God, and I had fed the doubting parts. I too had rushed into the "broad way"—the popular way—of my generation, the way of ideology and political theorizing, the way of psychology and scientific "positivism," the way of doubt and skepticism of all tradition and truth. Now I wanted to "return home" as these early Friends had done, to "own" the light again and be guided by it to a place of "true rest and peace." God had been pouring his spirit out on me my entire life, and I had not received him in a way I could build on, but now I would. I felt my heart respond to the idea of returning to Christ:

> *O that I might now be joined to him, and he alone might live in me!* And so, in the willingness which God had wrought in me, in this day of his power to my soul, I gave up to be instructed, exercised and led by him, in the waiting for and feeling of his holy seed, that all might be wrought out of me which could not live with the seed, but would be hindering the dwelling and reigning of the seed in me, while it remained and had power.[9]

This was the way back—waiting for and feeling for his "holy seed," listening for his voice to instruct me, seeing the things in me that "could not live with [it] but [that] hinder[ed] the dwelling and reigning of the seed in me." This was the way Friends pointed toward. It was just as present to us as it had been to Quakers in seventeenth-century England and to Christians in first-century Jerusalem.

But there was more to it than this. The interior Christ was not just a presence, not just an aura to be engulfed in. He was an active presence. He was in us in his crucifixion. He was in us in his birth. He was in us to redeem us, to save us, to bring us back into the image and likeness of God that we had been created to reflect. As Penington put it in one of his writings, "I have met with my Saviour; and he has not been present with me without his salvation, . . ."[10]

Salvation for Friends was at the heart of God's work in the world and in our lives. But salvation wasn't something far off or distant any more than God was. It wasn't something one came into only after death. It was something to be entered into now—not perhaps in its ultimate fullness, but in sufficient fullness for everything in and around us to be changed, and for the hope of a future perfection to be made real in us. Eternal life was not about before or after time for early Friends, or before or after the things in time. Eternal life was about coming into union with God by being joined to him in Christ. As John taught, "this is everlasting life, that they may know you, the only true God, and Jesus Christ whom you have sent" (17:3).

I didn't see all of this in the very beginning of the turn in me. But I did see that it was possible that Christ was present in this intimate and powerful interior way, and that if I opened myself to him there, he would guide me back to life. As I opened to seeing what was going on in me and in my journey with my friend in terms of the Christian story, I began to feel this work of salvation as well. Friends used different images to name Christ's presence and work: He is light, opening and illuminating the way God wants us to walk and the way he wants us to understand his gospel; He is God's word or voice, communicating to us God's will and letting us know the direction we should go in; He is God's holy seed, stirring in us, bursting through the hard ground of resistance in us and growing into a sheltering vine in which we can find life. These were the most common names Friends used to refer to Christ's indwelling Spirit. But there were others. He was our prophet, our high priest, our king, our messiah, our lamb, our shepherd. Virtually all of the redemptive images and figures that were part of the Scripture context pointed to some way that God's presence and power was in and among us to lead us to life.

The goal of Christ's saving work in us was to bring us out of "the fall"—the futility, alienation, and sin that ordinary life (life without faith) entailed. This fallenness was not some exotic state. It was the state of our ordinary lives when we tried to find our way without God. But salvation was more than about just our personal lives; there was a corporate dimension to salvation too—the creation of a kingdom-like order at least among those gathered into Christ—and an eternal dimension—the traditional vision of a heavenly state one could enter into after this life. The part I identified with most in the beginning of my journey was the personal, experiential dimension, the sense I had as I began to see the gospel in the way I have described, that the futility, confusion, and meaninglessness of my life was something faith could overcome.

The first and most exciting part of the salvation I felt open to me in the earliest days of my conversion or convincement was the simple joy I felt at finally being able to see what I had been blind to about Christ—being able to know what it meant to have Christ "dwell in [my] heart through faith" as Paul had said, to begin "to have the power to comprehend [. . .] the breadth and length and height and depth, and to know the love of Christ that surpasses knowledge, [. . .] (Eph. 17-19). To this day it is one of the chief joys I have as a Christian. But it was more than this. It was a journey, a way of walking in the light and power of Christ, hearing his voice, experiencing the good that flowed from obedience to him in all the little things that made up my life.

No sudden outward miracles attended my convincement, unless you count as I do the deep and invisible miracle convincement was itself. My outward life was not suddenly different, but inwardly everything was changed. I saw differently.

When I spoke to my friend of what was happening in me, I found myself using an image from a movie I knew and loved—the 1962 classic *The Miracle Worker* with Anne Bancroft and Patty Duke. The movie, based on a play by William Gibson, was about the young Helen Keller, a woman whose victory over blindness and deafness made her a celebrity in the early years of the twentieth century. The story is about the breakthrough that made it possible for her to learn human language and have access to all that language brings—knowledge of the world, ordered thought, and communication—everything that makes human beings what they are. Helen's teacher, Annie Sullivan, teaches her a tactile alphabet that makes it possible for Helen to learn words and language. Helen quickly learns the fingered alphabet and mimics the movement of her teacher's fingers to get items she knows and wants—her D-O-L-L, her M-O-T-H-E-R, the sweet C-A-K-E she loves. She enjoys playing the finger game and gets to be quite good at it. But the concept behind the game—the thing her teacher really wants her to get—the idea that everything can be named and that these words can make learning and communication with other human beings possible for her—this is something Helen cannot seem to grasp. For months Miss Sullivan labors to get the idea across with no success. But finally, as she is about to give up, Helen has a moment of grace at the water pump outside her parents' home. Forced to refill a pitcher of water she has intentionally dumped on her teacher, Helen holds the pitcher under the spout while Miss Sullivan pumps the water and spells the word W-A-T-E-R into her palm. Again and again, she pumps and spells. Finally it happens. Something in that moment at the pump—its intensity—its repetition—or its evocation of a primitive memory Helen has of a time when she still could see and hear and knew what water was—something, some grace sparks a light in Helen's mind and she "sees" what her teacher has been trying to open to her.

This was exactly what I felt was happening to me. I was seeing a landscape I had never really seen before, a landscape I had stumbled around in for years and knew in a superficial way but not in a way I'd been able to make sense of. The words that were penetrating my darkness and opening my spiritual condition to me were words I had toyed with for years, words of Christian faith—the light of Christ, the cross, resurrection, the "Word," the seed. But the words were more than just words. They were a set of contexts, a whole spiritual vocabulary rooted in the biblical story of Christ.

I embraced the opportunity to explore what faith could do. In the midst of all this, sometime in November of 1979, I received word from a school superintendent in Vancouver, British Columbia, that my son was there, enrolled in an elementary school in the city. I contacted an attorney there and proceeded with plans to go and retrieve him. By the end of November, he was home. While the next months would still be filled with tension and worry about further conflict, the worst was over. I could start to rebuild.

5

Learning the Landscape

The way you "see" shapes everything you do—how you interpret your inner life, how you view events, how you conduct yourself, relate to others, respond to issues, and make decisions. "The eye is the lamp of the body. [. . .] if your eye is healthy, your whole body will be full of light . . ." (Matt. 6:22). As I saw the landscape in me and around me that I had been blind to, I was seized with the same kind of thirst for it that Helen is seized with in *The Miracle Worker,* a thirst to explore it, to know the words that could open it, to see everything they could communicate. This wasn't the same Quakerism I had been around for years. I wanted to know more about early Friends, more about how they had understood the Christian gospel, more about how they had put their faith to work in their lives. The process was not instantaneous, but the rewards it brought from the very beginning were very great. The changes it helped me make in my life, the intense satisfaction it brought to my heart as I yielded to it, and the confirmation it seemed to give to the faith I had learned but then rejected gave me reasons to trust it in a way I had not been able to do earlier.

There were no outward miracles in the beginning of my spiritual journey with Christ. I certainly was not called into any of the kind of ministries we so often associate with conversion, things like feeding the hungry or helping the homeless. These things were too similar to the kinds of things I had spent my adult life concerned about as a political radical—not that we ever really fed the hungry or helped the homeless, but we agitated against the "system" we saw as causing their hunger and homelessness. Anyway, for a while I found it difficult to separate even genuine works of charity from my earlier efforts at social change.

There was in me a recoiling from the things that I had "fed," when I was famishing "that which desired after God" as Francis Howgill had said—the ideologies I had given myself to—the psychological theories, radical political ideas and the rigorous materialism I had seen as scientific. These had been my idols, the things I had used to keep me from God, things that had justified my lack of faith. Now I saw them as Jeremiah had seen the idols of his day, as "cracked cisterns that can hold no water" (Jer. 2:13).

My reaction was so strong that it would be years before I was able to feel any desire to be involved in political or social activism. I knew how dangerous such activism could be to spiritual growth and insight. The ideologies propelling the activism had credibility and stature in the modern world. They were the wind, earthquake, and fire around us that vie with the still voice of God in us, and I wanted no part of them any more. I confess now that I overreacted, but that was part of the journey.

What I did feel called to do was just to speak about what was happening to me. It wasn't easy to let people know that I had changed. Even with my own children I felt a sense of discomfort about bringing God into the conversation. I have noticed this in other people as well. They shrink from speaking in terms of their faith, even when it is at the heart of everything they think and do. But it wasn't just bringing God's name into the conversation. It was bringing a sense of God's reality and presence to bear on everything. It doesn't do any good to speak about God when you know people cannot hear the name spoken without thinking you foolish or crazy, or just dismissing you as irrelevant. You have to find ways of speaking his name and telling about his work in ways people can hear. I don't know how successful I was in this. I only know it was hard and is hard, but the advantage I brought to the task was that I knew what it was to be on the other side, to be alienated from God and talk of God, to put religious people into a category that didn't require me to try to understand them or really listen to them. What I am doing in this book is an extension of this call that I have felt from the beginning—trying to find a way to let people know that God is real and accessible, and that our religious traditions are vital and speak to our deepest human needs.

The most difficult and immediate issues I faced in the months immediately following the opening of my eyes to Christ had to do with my impending divorce and the relationship that was developing with my friend from Meeting. While my friend continued to feel sure that God wanted him to remain open to healing and reconciliation in his marriage, I had no such leading. I entertained the notion a time or two, but every time I did, I had the sense that doing anything that would communicate a change in my resolve would be a terrible test of the faith God was stirring in me, like leaping off a cliff to prove that I was in God's care. I had so many other things I had to deal with like stabilizing my children's lives, getting our finances under control, and figuring out how I was going to make a living for us. The search for my son and my trip up to Canada to retrieve him had put me deeply in debt, and the job I had held for two years was ending. I needed either to open a private law office or find another job somewhere. I also continued to worry that the conflict with my estranged husband might lead to further difficulties with him; inwardly I even feared the possibility of violence and turned to God very earnestly in these early months to ease my fears in this regard.

As far as the relationship with my friend was concerned, it continued to be a matter of trying to put our wills aside and let God work the matter out in his own time. The situation provided many opportunities for both of us to practice discernment and self-denial. The few surviving letters and notes that passed between us in early 1980 attest to the difficulty we sometimes had trying to be faithful in our beginnings. One note he sent me at the time included this extraordinary passage from an Isaac Penington devotional. It spoke powerfully to our condition:

> Do not look for such great matters to begin with; but be content to be a child, and let the Father proportion out daily to thee what light, what power, what exercises, what straits, what fears, what troubles he sees fit for thee and do thou bow before him continually in humility of heart. Thou must join in with the beginning of life, and be exercised with the day of small things before thou meet with the great things, wherein is the clearness and satisfaction of the soul. The rest is at noonday, but the travels begin at the breakings of day, wherein are but glimmerings of little light, wherein the discovery of good and evil are not so manifest and certain; yet THERE must the traveller begin and travel; and in his faithful travels the light will break in upon him more and more.[1]

This was true. The journey starts where you are, in whatever darkness and confusion you are in. To imagine that God will suddenly give you the power to work miraculous changes in your life or to undo the consequences of sins you have persisted in for years is to expect too much. It is to "run off" in your own will, thinking it is God's, following some notion you have about what God would have you do. Real faith doesn't look like that. Real faith in the beginning is only a tiny seed that has been much neglected. It is a seed with great potential and great promise, but it is still a seed. The important thing is to try in the small ways that are opened to you to move in the direction of the light that will make the seed grow. God does not expect extraordinary things from spiritual newborns. The life of faith is a journey; one doesn't just materialize at the finish line without first learning how to crawl, how to toddle, and then how to walk.

As for running, one could never aspire to that. Running was always seen as a bad thing in the thinking of early Friends. One couldn't keep in touch with one's guide when one ran.

> Thou must wait for life to be measured out by the Father and be content with what proportion, and at what time, he shall please to measure.
>
> Oh! be little, be little; and then thou wilt be content with little. And if thou feel now and then a check or a secret smiting—in *that* is the Father's love; be not over-wise or over-eager in thy own willing, running, and desiring, and thou mayst feel it so and by degrees come to the knowledge of thy Guide, who will lead

> thee, step by step, in the path of life and teach thee to follow and in his own season, powerfully judge that which cannot or will not follow. Be still, and wait for light and strength and desire not to know or comprehend, but to be known and comprehended in the love and life which seeks out, gathers, and preserves the lost sheep.[2]

But it isn't easy being little. The heroes of faith we celebrate—the prophets, martyrs, and saints—sometimes give us the impression that God is only interested in the great and memorable demonstrations of his power in our lives, but this is not true. The sturdy foundation in faith is built on faithfulness in the small things that make up the fabric of our lives—the integrity of words and deeds, our willingness to recognize and repair mistakes we make, our willingness to witness to his presence and authority in our lives—the small and very concrete ways we express the love he pours out on us. These were the things I felt most encouraged to work on.

In January of 1980, I had an opportunity to attend a conference in Pennsylvania of a Quaker group called New Foundation Fellowship, led by a man named Lewis Benson. Born a Friend in 1909, Benson discovered the writings of George Fox, founder of the Religious Society of Friends, early in his life, shortly after experiencing a Christian conversion similar in some respects to the conversion Fox had undergone. Benson had been amazed to learn how different Fox's message was from the message he had grown up with as a birthright Friend. By the late 1970s, he had become the leading authority on Fox and Fox's theology among Friends. The disparity between that theology and the relatively incoherent theology of twentieth-century Friends distressed him, so he made it his life's work to try to revive the Christian vision of Fox in the Society of Friends. New Foundation was only his latest effort to promote this mission.

The gathering was my first formal exposure to Fox's thought and to the kind of worship that could happen when everyone was gathered into the same vision of Christ. It was very inspiring. I had read a little of Fox in shorter pamphlets and collections of early Quaker writers, but now I became familiar with his journal. Because of the importance of Fox's vision to my own ideas and my own journey, I need to spend some time presenting his thought. To do that I must also touch a little on the historical context in which he lived.

Fox was born in 1624 in the midlands of England. To put that date into some historical context, 1624 was just a little over a hundred years after Luther posted his Ninety-five Theses on the door of the Wittenburg Church and just a little under a hundred years since England's Henry VIII had broken from Rome to start the Church of England. In that hundred years, England had suffered enormous religious turmoil. Henry's daughter Mary had tried to reestablish the Roman Catholic Church, burning at the stake some three hundred Protestants in the effort. Elizabeth I reversed her sister's work and reestablished the Protestant church along more "moderate" lines—keeping a good deal of the Catholic pageantry and hierarchical structure while moving away from Catholic dogmas a bit more than her father had. At the same time all these religious changes were taking place, the economic and political stability of the country was also being shaken to the core, a shaking that brought forth numerous splinter groups of religious dissenters. The dissenters had radical ideas about the shape England's social and political structure should assume. By the time Fox was born, religious tolerance had gained a modest foothold in England, but radical Protestants and Catholics were still subject to persecution—loss of property, jailing, whipping, branding, and other trials. The brutality and persistence of religious conflict in the sixteenth and seventeenth centuries would ultimately bring about an antireligious reaction with the coming of the Enlightenment, but Fox lived in the turmoil just before, a period of radical religious thought and millenarian expectations. Fox was sixteen when the English Civil War broke out. He was twenty-five when Charles I was put to death by the Puritan faction of the English Parliament.

Fox describes himself in his journal as an ardent Christian from his earliest years, but his devotion to Christ and his constant reading of the Scriptures did not bring him happiness. This depressed and distressed him. At nineteen, he left home to seek out someone who could give him advice or guide him, encourage him, and help him achieve the kind of peace he thought the gospel of Christ promised to believers. He visited everyone he thought might be able to help—all the "experts" in religion—but no one could help him. His relatives tried to get him to find a wife and settle down, but he was persistent. After a few years, he began to have what he called "openings" into the gospel and the Scriptures—things he felt clear and certain about. He realized, for example, that a true believer in Christ is not just someone who calls himself a Christian, but one who has in some way "passed from death to life" [3]; that being a real "minister of Christ"[4] meant more than just getting a degree at a university; and "that God, who made the world, [really] did not dwell in temples made with hands [. . .] but in people's hearts."[5]

Then, sometime in the year 1647, when he was twenty-three, Fox had a powerful personal experience of God's presence. He described it as a voice saying "There is one, even Christ Jesus, that can speak to thy condition [. . . and] when I heard it my heart did leap for joy."[6] It is hard at first to understand why these words had such revelatory power for Fox. He already believed that God dwelled in human hearts, and he already knew that Christ was the center of his faith. But what he experienced was not an intellectual idea but an experience of God's voice opening Christ's presence to him in a very immediate way. Fox's experience of Christ's voice and presence in him were not the end of his seeking, any more than they would be for me centuries later. It was the beginning. For several years after this opening, Fox continued struggling with the temptations and worldly habits that kept him from entering into Christ's peace. But he finally did come into a state of mind and heart so settled and so sure of Christ's support that he described it as a kind of reentry into paradise. The idea that a Christian could come into such a blessed state in this life outraged many contemporaries of Fox, who believed as a matter of doctrine that man could never overcome sin in this life but had to wait for God's reward of peace in heaven. Fox didn't mean by his claim that all the outward incidences of life could be perfect—he suffered many outward hardships over the course of his later life—but he never retracted his statement that believers could come into a state of spiritual restoration in this life. In fact, many of the "testimonies" Friends later became famous for flowed directly from the conviction that they could.

The theology Fox articulated to explain his insights and experiences was not unorthodox. The ecclesiological (church-related) conclusions he drew were—very—but the Christology he adopted was fairly mainstream. Fox explained his experience of Christ's presence in himself and in others as a fulfillment of two Old Testament prophecies: the promise that a prophet like Moses would come in the future (Deut. 18:15–19) and the promise that a new covenant would be instituted by this new Moses (Jer. 31:31–34).

The Deuteronomy prophesy reads,

> The Lord your God will raise up for you a prophet like me [Moses] from among your own people. [. . .] Anyone who does not heed the words that the prophet shall speak in my name, I myself will hold accountable.

That Christ was this new Moses was not an idea unique to Fox. It was very much a part of the vision the New Testament gospel writers had of Christ. Matthew, in particular, develops the view that Christ is this promised prophet. Like Moses, he is threatened with extinction in childhood by a tyrannical ruler (2:13); he is called out of Egypt to go to the land of Israel (2:19–21); he is tempted in the wilderness for forty days and nights as Moses and the people were tempted for forty years (4:2); and he gives his new law to the people from up on a mountain rather than down on a plain as recounted in Luke. The fact that his new law is not one primarily concerned with outward observances but inward, heart-related realities brings out the connection Matthew also seeks to draw to the Jeremiah prophesy:

> The days are surely coming, says the Lord, when I will make a new covenant with the house of Israel and the house of Judah. It will not be like the covenant that I made with their ancestors when I took them by the hand to bring them out of the land of Egypt—a covenant that they broke, though I was their husband, [. . .] But this is the covenant that I will make [. . .] I will put my law within them, and I will write it on their hearts; and I will be their God, and they shall be my people. No longer shall they teach one another, or say to each other, "Know the Lord," for they shall all know me, from the least of them to the greatest, [. . .] for I will forgive their iniquity, and remember their sin no more.

Christ had come not only to die for our sins but also to bring this new covenant into being. The law would be established in human hearts when the Holy Spirit came:

> "Those who love me will keep my word, and my Father will love them, and we will come to them and make our home with them.[. . .] But the Advocate, the Holy Spirit, whom the Father will send in my name, will teach you everything, and remind you of all that I have said to you" (John 14:23, 25).

The inward teacher, alluded to in Jeremiah's prophesy, was this Advocate, this Spirit. John also refers to it as the anointing:

> [. . .] the anointing that you received from him abides in you, and so you do not need anyone to teach you. But as his anointing teaches you about all things, and is true and is not a lie, and just as it has taught you, abide in him (1 John 2:27).

This anointing or Advocate—the Holy Spirit—was the voice that spoke in Fox, and the voice that spoke in all who sought to be guided by God. Again, none of this was new theology. The prophecies of Moses and Jeremiah were not excluded from the list of prophecies that had been fulfilled in Christ from the point of view of Christian believers, but Fox drew conclusions from these prophecies that other Christians had not and that certainly the church had not. Here I would include in my definition of church not only the ancient historic churches (Catholic and Orthodox) but also Reformation churches. If Christ *within* was to be our teacher, if the law and way of life he had instituted was so accessible that they "no longer [needed to] teach one another [to] know the Lord . . . ," then why had the faith remained so wedded to outward things, to complicated doctrinal statements, elaborate sacraments, and outward practices? Fox concluded that all of this was way off base (what he called apostate) and had been for nearly the entire span of the church's existence—sixteen hundred years. Christ's coming, he said, had meant to bring to a close the time of outward law and outward religious observance, not just the outward practice of circumcision and temple sacrifice. The church had not been faithful. Its leaders had not trusted in God's anointing to teach and bring believers into communion, but had fallen back on outward forms and rituals—Christianized forms perhaps, but outward all the same: baptism, communion, ordination of priests, liturgies, even the outward letter of Scripture. By the outward letter, Fox meant the kind of "cookbook" approach to Scripture he felt the Reformed churches were guilty of.

Fox rejected all of these—not the inward realities represented by them, but the outward acts or practices meant to embody them. His rejection of outward observances didn't mean that everyone was on his own to decide what was true, however, or that there was no communal dimension of church life. Fox was not an anarchist. The New Covenant gospel gathered people and kept order among them even without these outward things, an order he called "gospel order." It was to keep "gospel order" that Fox established Monthly Meetings and Yearly Meetings that would handle issues that arose and test controversial leadings people claimed to have from Christ.

The fact that this radically inward approach to the gospel, which he considered the "true" gospel of Christ had never been preached, as far as Fox was aware, at any point in Christian history did not sway him from believing it was true. It made him think that he might be playing a part in the end time story described so mysteriously and symbolically in Revelation. Fox thought that his recovery and reproclamation of this long lost gospel might actually bring about the culmination of history that the first-century church had expected. Maybe the Second Coming had not occurred because the preaching of the gospel had not gone forward as faithfully as it was meant to have gone. For a time, it seems possible that Fox believed it might come in his day, inasmuch as he was preaching the gospel Christ had wanted preached sixteen hundred years earlier. So Fox went out and preached his radical version of the gospel, and thousands were gathered in months. Quakerism spread like wildfire in its first years.

Fox saw his mission as calling people off the outward things that the "judaisers"[7] in the church had instituted and pointing them toward their true teacher, the inward Christ:

> [. . .] the Lord Christ Jesus was come to teach his people himself and bring them off all the world's ways and teachers to Christ,

> their way to God; and I laid open all their teachers and set up the true teacher, Christ Jesus; and how they were judged by the prophets, Christ, and the apostles; and to bring them off the temples made with hands, that they themselves might know they were the temples of God.[8]

The despair people struggled with as Christians worrying about their souls, fretting about whether or not they were saved, not being able to come into a state of spiritual rest or peace came from being caught up in useless and empty forms and forgetting that the covenant of Christ was inward and real and full of power. People had forgotten the spring of water that was bubbling within them:

> Oh, when will you be weary of feeding on the wind, and of husks among swine, and on that which dies of itself? And when will you inquire after the living God, who is power? How long have you talked of his power to come? Many years. You are still as far off, if not further, than you were before. You have told of the glory of the Lord to be revealed, and of his law being written in the heart, and of God teaching his people himself, and of his spirit being poured out on his sons and daughters; and you cannot see that you have obtained nothing.[9]

Friends were determined not to make the same mistake. As people responded to Fox's message and were gathered together in community, the "form" of worship they instituted was a corporate silence, where everyone waited on the Spirit to open God's word to them, to speak that word as led and to come into the peace and rest of God. But the elimination of outward forms, complete as it was, did not mean that Friends rejected the historical reality of Jesus' coming as Christ or the basic truths contained in the creeds. It was not a rejection of the fundamental revelation contained in the Scriptures. The truth as Fox and early Friends saw it was incoherent and inconceivable without these things. This, of course did not stop his seventeenth-century opponents from saying that Fox denied Christ, the creeds, and Scripture. In 1671, Fox and Quaker leaders issued a letter denying these slanders formally, but the slanders continued.[10]

So this was the theological content of Fox's approach to the gospel of Christ. Despite the years that had passed from the seventeenth century to modern times, Fox's approach seemed very relevant to those of us gathered at the New Foundation conference. What appealed to us in it were his Christ-centeredness, his close connection with and comprehension of the Scriptures, and the spiritual power the message unleashed in the faith community gathered into it. We recognized the differences between his time and ours, but the things he had discovered about Christ's closeness and Christ's power to transform lives were things we had discovered too. The fact that he had come to these truths in a super-religious environment that veiled the living Christ behind an excess of outwardness—constant dispute over observances, doctrines, and church order—while we had come to them in an environment that veiled Christ behind a wall of religious indifference and doubt did not seem critically important to us. What we had in common was an experience of having penetrated a thick veil to come into the living Christ.

We didn't spend much time worrying about whether Fox's analysis of Christian history was completely correct. If I had asked myself that question then, I probably would have said no, that his "take" on it was too extreme, that he wasn't really rediscovering a gospel that had been lost. He was simply focusing on an "aspect" or "dimension" of the gospel that had been neglected. What Friends involved in New Foundation wanted to do was let Friends know the fullness of the gospel in which Quakerism was rooted. They thought that if other Friends could only hear it and experience the power in it, they too would see how central Christ was.

I left the conference optimistic about the state of things in the Society of Friends. There were challenges, but there were also people responding to those challenges and eager to preach the word about Christ.

6

Friends and the Scriptures

If the most important thing I got from early Friends was a quickening of my faith in Christ, the second was a sense of the importance of Scripture's words, images, and contexts in helping me to see the spiritual dimension of my own life. As I've said, the words and contexts of Scripture seemed to me a kind of spiritual "alphabet" that was able to give people access to a world we were naturally blind to—as the tactile alphabet Helen Keller used had given her access to the world she lived in but could not see. From the moment my faith was revived, the Scriptures took on great importance to me, and the approach early Friends took to the Scriptures became one of my chief interests.

Modern Friends believe that Quakers were different from other Reformation-era Protestants in the degree of authority they ascribed to the Scriptures in that they put a distance between themselves and Scripture that the others did not. This is only superficially true, however. It is true that early Friends refused to call the Bible "God's Word." Christ was God's Word. The Scriptures were "merely" God's words, words that had been brought forth by his Spirit in the past. The "letter of Scripture" was therefore not as authoritative as other Protestants insisted. God's Spirit was the ultimate authority. Fox also denied that the truths he had come to about Christ were things he had learned from reading the Bible. He wrote in his journal that the things that God had "opened to him" about Christ had come to him not "by the help of man, nor by the letter [of Scripture], though they are written in the letter, but I saw them in the light of the Lord Jesus Christ, and by his immediate Spirit and power, as did the holy men of God, by whom the Holy Scriptures were written."[1] As I said, statements like this one seemed to put distance between the believer and the book. But when you look behind them to how Friends actually used the Scriptures, you see something much more complex, much more interesting.

Scripture was not the "container" of God's spirit; it was a fruit of the Spirit's work in God's people, a uniquely important fruit. Instead Friends tried to get people to apply Scripture to their own lives, "their own states," as Fox says in his journal.[2] The characters of Scripture were not just historical personages. They were exemplars of all kinds of human conditions and attitudes. Those who envied and persecuted the godly were people who dwelled in "the nature of Cain," for example; or those who chose earthly goods over the heavenly promises of God were like Esau. Even "things" in the Scripture could represent human states. I think, for example, of the way William Penn used the image of the overcrowded inn in Bethlehem to illuminate the spiritual condition of the average person's soul, too full of worldly guests to receive Christ in us:

> Like the inn of old, thou hast been full of other guests: thy affections have entertained other lovers: there has been no room for thy Saviour in thy soul.[3]

Or Fox's use of John the Baptist's proclamation as a description of how hearts are readied to receive Christ by having the mountainous barriers to faith laid low in them and the lowly valleys of faith raised up:

> And I saw the mountains burning up and the rubbish and the rough and crooked ways and places made smooth and plain that the Lord might come into his tabernacle. These things are to be found in man's heart. But to speak of these things being within seemed strange to the rough and crooked and mountainous ones.[4]

Both of these images I responded to. I had experienced what it was like to be so full of *worldly* ways of looking at life that I had no room in me for Christ to be born. I had felt the mountains of skepticism and ideology laid low in me as the frail valleys of faith were raised up.

But while examples of this kind of biblical allusion or symbolism are common in the writings of early Friends, what Friends ultimately saw in Scripture was something far more profound. They saw that the whole story of Scripture recapitulated itself in the lives of people who opened themselves to Christ and became joined to him by faith. If one came to a faith that was like the faith of Scripture, a daily faith in God's guidance, the spiritual journey one would find oneself on would actually parallel the story Scripture told—or at least its key events. The story was not Adam's alone or the Jews' alone. It was the common spiritual heritage of all men and women. *We* were the ones cast out of God's presence, the ones who envied and killed our brothers, who wandered the world in alienation from God and strangers to one another. We were the ones who had to respond to God's call and learn to rely on the word God addressed to us. As we did that, as we did what Abraham did, we too would be brought into the holy land that was God's to bestow—not in outward detail but in spiritual substance. Early Friends saw themselves in these terms. They often described themselves as "spiritual Jews" being rescued from bondage and led to freedom, as in the following passage:

> . . . now it [pleased] the divine being in his infinite love and tender pity and compassion to look down upon us, whilst in the land of Egypt, and house of bondage spiritually, and to send forth his light and truth, to give us a sense inwardly of the deplorable states of our souls in the separation from, and depravation of the enjoyments of the Lord, which sense and sight begat in us living breathings and a holy cry after the knowledge of him we saw ourselves ignorant of . . .[5]

Or they saw themselves as spiritually dead people raised from the dead just as Jesus was raised. Scripture allusion gave power to their description of their own experiences:

> Wait to see the law set up within . . . and the rebellious nature yoked [earthquakes and thunder]. Wait in patience for the judgment, and let the Lord's work have its perfect operation in you; and so as you turn to him who has smitten and wounded you; he will bind up and heal. And give up all to the great slaughter of the Lord, to the Cross. . . . And as the earth comes to be plowed up, the seed which is sown comes up; and, the rocks broken, the water gushes out. You so will see that some promises will arise in you to the Seed which is coming up out of the grave, and so the love of God will appear in you, and you will be stayed, and see hope in the midst of calamity.
>
> And as you come to be redeemed from under the bondage of sin, and come above the bonds of death, and the pure principle lives in you, there will be a delight in you to do the will of the father, who has redeemed you from sin and its law to righteousness and its law, . . .[6]

This was what they meant when they said you had to enter into the Spirit that gave the Scriptures forth to "see" the true meaning of the words there and to see the same work carried forth in your own life.

Fox saw the Scripture story as involving a sequence of "ministrations" (steps or phases of God's ministering work). He believed that he himself had passed through a process of redemption substantially the same as what had happened in the history recorded in Scripture, and he told his story in terms of these ministrations. I have already touched on Fox's life a little in presenting his theology, but I will show here how he used the idea of these stages or ministrations.

The "ministration of condemnation" was the first. In this ministration, the real truth of our spiritual condition in the fall is opened to us inwardly; it is a condition of spiritual darkness and death. It is characteristically the first opening of Christ's light in the mind and heart of the seeker. It can be distinguished from despair by the fact that it is always accompanied in some measure by a sense of Christ's loving presence and power to overcome the death in which one is caught. It is Christ's light that illuminates the dark landscape, so his presence is presupposed. In Fox's own journey he sees himself entering this ministration when he sees that people "[do] not possess what they profess"—indeed that even he does not.[7] The problem is deeper than hypocrisy. The problem is that people are alienated from the very power that can help them possess or live out the truths they profess. In this ministration, Fox sees the gulf that separates him from God and wants to bridge it. He knows about the Christ of Scripture, and he knows about the Christ of church doctrine and teaching, but he does not yet know Christ as a presence and power in him that can lead him out of the darkness.

The "ministration of Moses" is the next stage. This is the time of crying out to God, of being led out of the "world" (i.e. Egypt, the flesh, bondage, death) and into a wilderness ("that which is not world"[8]) where we can learn to discern what must be left behind and what may be kept. In this ministration, we also come to see our transgressions through what Fox calls "the pure law of God," a law that is now written on the heart. This law is not to be done away with but clung to and obeyed; the time of trial and judgment under it must be endured.

In Fox's own story, the ministration of Moses begins for him when he heads out to look for that wise or "expert" Christian who can help him discover why he is caught in the dilemma of not being able to possess what he professes. The earliest stages of this ministration might well have been called the ministration of Abraham, for it involves an Abraham-like break from the religious traditions of the past, the spiritually empty, formal religion that Fox believed we all started from but that some mistakenly cling to as "truth." Like Abraham, we will be blessed when we obey God's voice and abandon these traditions and seek God's living presence.[9]

All Fox's major "openings" are experienced in the ministration of Moses. Through these openings or revelations, he realizes that he must move from the "fleshly" understanding to which he is accustomed to a more spiritual grasp of God's work in his life. It is the process of being weaned away from the "common belief of people" that characterizes the openings he has during this stage. The openings he experiences here lead him to rely less and less on those thought to be spiritually wise by worldly standards and more on the sense of what God seems to be saying within him. He begins to see what the new covenant is all about—that believers ". . . needed no man to teach them, but as the anointing teacheth them. . . ."[10] Finally he experiences the opening concerning Christ's inward presence, which I quoted earlier. This is, of course, always the quote that Christian Friends use to describe what it is that Friends believe, that Jesus Christ dwells in the human heart and that it is he who teaches and speaks to the condition of every person. But in Fox's account, what this opening reveals is simply the identity of the light that has been guiding him all along. He is still only somewhere in the middle of the ministration of Moses when he has this opening, and it will be years before he emerges from the desert in which his soul is journeying. He has not yet even begun his passage through the law.

The journey through the wilderness looks to our worldly mind as if it should be short and direct, but in truth it is long and often circuitous. It is not a journey of miles, but of mileposts that are spiritual. We must just go on in childlike trust, seeking God's presence in the most personal way. It requires great patience to endure the testing and purging process that constitutes the work of the law. Fox sees the law of Moses, which Christians tend to dismiss as unimportant in the ministration of Christ, as essential to the progress of the soul. He does not see it as outward law but as a pure spiritual fire that burns up all that is contrary to God's will. The painful inner discernment Fox feels throughout this ministration is the work of the law in him, a law that must be passed through to get to the ministration of the prophets and of Christ:

> The pure and perfect law of God is over the flesh to keep it and its works, which are not perfect, under, by the perfect law; and the law of God that is perfect answers the perfect principle of God in every one. . . . None knows the giver of this law but by the spirit of God, neither can any truly read it or hear its voice but by the spirit of God.[11]

It is the spirit of repentance that is brought forth by the pure law testified to by the prophets and John the Baptist, and it too must be passed through before one can come to a participation in the cross of Christ. Going through the judgment due under the pure law of God is a painful time for Fox, as it is for all men, but as he permits God to exercise his just judgment over all that denies his Spirit, he passes through the ministration of the law to the ministration of the prophets and of John the Baptist who sees to the fulfillment promised in Christ:

> I saw this law was the pure love of God which was upon me, and which I must go through, though I was troubled while I was under it; for I could not be dead to the law but through the law which did judge and condemn that which is to be condemned. I saw many talked of the law, who had never known the law to be their schoolmaster; and many talked of the Gospel of Christ, who had never known life and immortality brought to light in them by it. . . . as you are brought into the law, and through the law to be dead to it, and witness the righteousness of the law fulfilled in you, ye will afterwards come to know what it is to be brought into the faith, and through faith from under the law. And abiding in the faith which Christ is the author of, ye will have peace and access to God.[12]

In this passage, we see one of the difficulties Fox's approach to Scripture involves—his deeply christocentric view of the Old Testament. It can be confusing to try to follow him, for even though he sees the ministrations as leading only gradually to the knowledge of Christ, he tends to mix and mingle Old Testament story with New Testament language and Christology.[13] Having, by the time of recounting his own story, passed through all the ministrations, Fox sees in all of them the Johannine Christ who is with God in the beginning and active *throughout* the entire story even when his face is hidden. He is in the promise to Eve—the "seed" of the woman that will bruise the head of the serpent and the voice that leads Abraham away from his ancestral land. He is the manna that feeds the Israelites in the desert and the pure law that Moses transmits to his people. He is the Word who speaks through the prophets and prepares the way for the incarnate Christ. Fox was not a systematic thinker or writer, so the boundaries of the various ministrations sometimes blur in his retelling. But these elements of potential confusion do not detract from the power of Fox's insights when we remember that he was trying to communicate about things not really susceptible to clear and logical explanation. Sometimes neat, linear concepts are just not adequate to point to spiritual truth.

It takes about five years from the time Fox begins his pilgrimage in the ministration of condemnation to the point where he passes through the ministration of John the Baptist, the last of the prophets, and enters into the very life and power of Christ, an experience he describes as a kind of combination of coming up out of slavery, a resurrection from the dead, and a restoration to the state Adam was in before he fell. It is the veritable reentry into paradise.

> Now was I come up in spirit through the flaming sword into the paradise of God. All things were new, and all the creation gave another smell unto me than before, beyond what words can utter. I knew nothing but pureness, and innocency, and righteousness, being renewed up into the image of God by Christ Jesus, so that I say I was come up to the state of Adam which he was in before he fell.[14]

Fox's account reflects spiritually the entire redemption narrative, from fall to restoration. He was convinced that everyone who opened to the spirit of Christ in them would find themselves involved in a journey like this, one that patterned itself after the events of the Scripture narrative. But until one entered personally on that journey, the Scripture narrative was not something one could really penetrate.

Of course, the passage of individual believers from condemnation to restoration was not all that the Scripture story told of or promised. It also goes forward to tell of the final gathering of God's faithful and the establishment of his kingdom on earth—things Christian believers had always believed Christ would bring to pass in his Second Coming. But while these times might not have yet come in history, the parallel spiritual event they represented could be experienced by the faithful in this life. The "Day of the Lord" itself was a kind of microcosmic recapitulation of the whole redemption trajectory—a coming of Christ's light, the pain of seeing our great separation from God, Christ's judgment, and the purgatorial, cleansing fires of his presence bringing us to God.

The movement through the various ministrations or stages of the redemption journey was not something that pertained only to individuals. The believing community could also experience the story in a spiritual way. When people criticized Fox for allowing women to preach or prophesy, for example, he routinely cited Joel's famous end-time prophecy for justification:

> "In the last days it will be, God declares, that I will pour out my Spirit upon all flesh, and your sons and your daughters shall prophesy. . . . Even upon my slaves, both men and women, in those days I will pour out my Spirit; and they shall prophesy" (Acts 2:17–18).

As I have already noted, Fox may well have seen the rapid gathering of Friends in response to his preaching as the beginning of the historical last days, days that had been delayed because of the early apostasy in the church. Fox scholars may debate this, but what Fox clearly believed was that the Scripture story operated on several different levels—historical, individual, and corporate. Scripture was not an artifact of God's work in the past or a static blueprint of what believers should believe. It was a dynamic story that recapitulated itself wherever God's spirit worked unhindered in the individual heart and among those gathered unto God on earth.

I spend this amount of time describing Fox's understanding of the redemption process as paralleling the Scripture story because it was to be so very important in my own understanding of the faith. Of all the unique insights Friends were to bring me, this one proved most influential in my own journey. I don't think most Friends, Christian or otherwise, attach this kind of importance to Fox's approach to the Scriptures. They prefer to pick out of Fox's account isolated insights or "openings" and treat these insights as if they were philosophical premises from which the distinctive Quaker practices or testimonies flow. But this was not the way Fox's mind worked. He believed that if one was being led by the same light that had led the holy men and women of God in history, one's journey would be similar. It was the similarity of the journey that let you know you were on the right path. God's truth is not changeable.

I wasn't sure that everything Fox said about the journey was accurate, but the general idea seemed convincing to me. The little bit of the journey I had been on seemed consistent with this general trajectory. I had known the "ministration of condemnation." Just about the first thing faith taught me was that sin was something real in my life. As is probably true with most modern people, I had never attached much validity to the concept of sin. People might do bad things because they were ignorant or neurotic or warped in some way as a result of bad experiences, but not because they were sinners. But now I began to see what sin was in me. I felt embarrassed about how willfully I had resisted God's kindnesses to me in my life, but even more than this I was aware of the sin wrapped around my relationship with my estranged husband. The sin there was not just in the ending of my marriage, but in the beginning of it, in the terrible self-centeredness of my thinking in those years. I had not really loved the man I had married. I had put my own security above his needs and legitimate expectations. I had brought children into a situation that was unstable and unhappy. I had never dealt with the underlying problems. I had threatened to leave a time or two, but I had never talked things out with my husband or sought help from anyone else. I had just let things build up until I couldn't stand the thought of dealing with them any more. Persisting in the relationship would not have done away with the sin. The sin was entangled in it too deeply.

Fox and early Friends understood this "ministration of condemnation." The consciousness of sin was central to the conversion process:

> *The first way of meeting with the Spirit of God, is as a convincer of sin.* Here is the true entrance; this is the key that opens into life eternal; he that can receive it, let him. It is not by soaring aloft into high imaginations and forms of worship; but by coming down to this low thing. This is the first and most proper work of the Spirit of God toward fallen man, whereby he makes way toward the writing of God's law in the heart; namely, to convince of sin.[15]

The awareness of sin I had was not a morbid thing. The very fact that it had been Christ's light that had shown me my fault made me know that the road ahead would be different, that he would help me learn what God wanted me to do, what I needed to change to come into his peace. He would be there in the cloud by day and the pillar of fire by night, in the manna I knew I needed to make the journey.

The idea that somehow the biblical story was a story that replicated itself in the individual spirit was something that struck me as positively modern, like Freud's approach to the ancient Oedipus story or the idea I had heard discussed in college biology that "ontogeny recapitulated phylogeny"—that the development of individual organisms recapitulates the development of the whole group of related organisms.

Why couldn't the Scripture narrative be a kind of archetype of the redemption experience? If God *did exist* and *did work* to redeem his creation, and if God *was* the same yesterday, today, and tomorrow, then why should his way of working that redemption *not* be manifest both in history and in the inner lives of people who opened themselves to him? The fact that the historical accounts of Scripture were not exactly the kind of history modern secular historians would produce, or the fact that there were undoubtedly elements of myth or legend mixed in with these accounts, did not interfere with their archetypal value. Even those parts that were merely "literature" might be true in that sense.

The multiple levels of use Fox made of the Scriptures was one of the most appealing things I found about him and early Friends. There might be things I disagreed with him about or thought were not relevant to our age, but his approach to the Scriptures was not one of them. The sense I had of Scriptures' absolutely essential role in bringing me into the Quaker vision of Christ and its usefulness in understanding the spiritual journey I saw myself as being on were undeniable as far as I was concerned. I could never prove that the events of Scripture were historically valid or accurate in a scientific sense, but the interior dimension I found there seemed trustworthy. It wasn't long before I began to trust the writings. I wasn't looking to them for history or science; I was looking to them for deeper truths. As I see it now, the very fact that the Bible exists as it does and has such continuing power to open God's presence and nature and work among us makes it something commensurate with the greatness we ascribe to God.

7

Friends' Testimonies

The radically inward New Covenant theology of early Friends brought forth among them a whole different way of pursuing the Christian life, a unique testimony that was and continues to be deeply meaningful to me. The central principle of Quaker spirituality was the mandate to "possess" what Christians had always "professed" and to possess it with sincerity of heart. As Fox wrote to his followers,

> I do charge you all in the presence of the living God to dwell in what you speak and profess. None to profess what he does not dwell in and none to profess what he is not; a sayer, and not a doer.[1]

Friends' success in doing this over the years has inspired respect for them among people everywhere, even people who know little about them. Their reputation for integrity and spiritual earnestness continues to this day. Modern Friends, even when they do not know or care much about what the earliest Friends thought theologically, respect the "testimonies"[2] they brought forth, among them simplicity, integrity, plain-speaking, equality of persons and the peace testimony. It is these testimonies that draw new attenders and members to the Society of Friends. It is what drew me in the years before my convincement. But the testimonies that have come down are not quite what they once were. They are not rooted in the same vision. In a way they have come down as "forms," as venerated customs or patterns of Quaker practice that seem beyond question. In this chapter I want to focus on the testimonies, the way early Friends "possessed" what they "professed," how they have come down to the modern era and how and to what extent they were meaningful to me.

Staying in Touch: Worship in Spirit and in Truth

Early Friends started from the premise that the outward forms of religion were powerless to bring believers into the real "enjoyments" of Christ's resurrected life—his peace, his holiness, and his victory over the world. But if professing creeds, participating in the sacraments, and obeying church ordinances could not bring believers into the promise, then what could? Only devotion to the inward Christ could do that—learning to hear and obey his voice in all things.

Doing this required that Friends stay in constant and dynamic "touch" with his presence in them, so that the law he had come to write on our hearts might be discerned and obeyed. Like Michelangelo's great painting of the creator God holding out his hand to the man he had created in his likeness, human life in its fullness consists in keeping touch with that hand, cultivating a sensitivity to that light and word, and becoming ever more rooted in that God's redeeming power.

But this place in us where God dwells is a place easily buried under the distracting clutter of worldly concerns, both material and immaterial. To see Christ in our hearts and minds and to draw from his presence the power to be obedient to his word requires a very special kind of spiritual discipline, a discipline that involves stillness, humility, attentiveness, and lots of patience. It also requires community and a connection with Scripture.

Christ's Spirit is always in us, but our openness and readiness to receive it is very variable. There are times when his touch is easy to perceive and powerful in its operation on our wills, as well as times when he seems distant and dreadfully silent. Our task is not necessarily to assume we're in touch but to try to be open to that touch when it is there and patient in waiting for it when it isn't:

> . . . the very sum of . . . true religion . . . [is] either to worship in the Spirit, or to wait for the Spirit. He who hath not received the Spirit, he is to wait for the Spirit. He who hath received the Spirit, he is to wait in the Spirit for the movings and outgoings thereof, and to be obedient thereto. And Christians are to take heed, not only of a wrong spirit, but also of quenching the movings of the true Spirit in themselves or others.[3]

Worship "in spirit and in truth" for early Friends was dedicated to the development of this discipline. If there was ever an "outward sacrament" instituted by Friends, it was the expectant silence of the Meeting for Worship. Here the concrete silencing of self and the shutting out of the world is achieved so that the inward grace they knew was available to all who came to the inner spring of eternal life could be received. There was no liturgy, no singing, no Scripture reading, no corporate prayer, no communion—nothing to distract the mind from the Teacher within. Still, Meeting for Worship was not an empty space but one rich in spiritual context. Meeting for Worship was the place where Friends came to know Christ in all his "offices," all those modes of his presence, all those "figures" of divinity that were gathered into his person:

> It is a glorious pasture, to be fed a-top of all the mountains in the Life . . . by the living Shepherd, to be overseen by the living Bishop and to be sanctified and . . . presented to God by the living Priest . . . by an everlasting Priest, that sanctifies and offers you to God without spot or wrinkle, a perfect offering. . . .
>
> Now you have an everlasting Preacher, whom God has anointed to preach, an everlasting Minister, that ministers Grace, Life, Salvation and Truth to you, an everlasting Prophet that God has raised up, who is to be heard; all the living hear him . . . So, none can silence or stop the mouth of them, whom he opens, or take away your Shepherd, your Bishop, your Minister, your Preacher, your Prophet, your Counsellor, etc. . . . Therefore, let him have your ears. Hearken to him. Let him be set up in your hearts . . .[4]

Friends sat quietly together to await the inward ministry of this Christ. If one *tried* to do anything in Meeting, it was to lay aside the "world" and the self and everything that flowed from them—worries, plans, notions, schemes, desires, grudges—everything that kept you from being attentive to the heavenly will that was not your own. But worship was not just silence; it was a silence in which everything Christ was could be sought after and savored. It was an expectant silence, for anyone might be "chosen" as a vehicle for Christ's ministry to the group. If you were "favored," the Spirit might give you something to offer those assembled, something to inspire or strengthen them, or something that simply assured them God was present among them. This kind of ministry was called vocal ministry and was thought to be really from Christ, not from the person who was the vehicle. A 1656 advice from Quaker elders in England reads,

> Ministers to speak the word of the Lord from the mouth of the Lord, without adding or diminishing. If anything is spoken out of the light so that "the seed of God" comes to be burdened, it is to be dealt with in private and not in the public meetings, "except there be a special moving to do so."[5]

The silence of the Meeting for Worship is something that has come down through the years in the "unprogrammed" tradition that is mostly followed in the Eastern United States,[6] and it remains what it always was, a place where you can encounter Christ. But people bring to the Meeting the expectations and theologies they have. If you bring to it an expectation of meeting Christ, you will meet him there. If you come expecting something less, that is what you will encounter. Meetings today seldom expect to encounter what early Friends expected, so the ministry you hear is very different.

The feeling of being called to give vocal ministry is a very powerful experience. As I became regular in my attendance at Meeting for Worship and grew in my understanding of what I was doing and expecting, I found myself called more and more to speak. The feeling was always the same—the burdened feeling, the feeling in my throat, the beating of my heart. These experiences understood in the light of Friends' theology were very special to me—like brushing the hem of Christ's garment inwardly.

By all accounts, the early Meetings of Friends were rich in spoken ministry—inspired prayer, teaching, and encouragement. But there were also times when Friends spoke and "outran" the Spirit. Being attentive meant learning when you were not being called. If you were not being moved by God to speak, you were supposed to remain silent, even if what you had to say seemed very interesting or wise to you. Friends were eloquent in describing and exhorting each other to self-restraint and attentiveness, as I have pointed out in the 1656 advice quoted above. The experience of being called to vocal ministry is not self-inflating. Far from generating pride, the idea that you might be "God's mouth" in some small way generates a deep humility:

> . . . stand still in quietness and meekness, that the still voice you may hear, which till you come down within, you cannot hear. . . . So be low and still, if you will hear his voice, and wait to hear that speak that separates between the precious and the vile, now that which you must wait in is near you, yes, in you.[7]

Worship was and continues to be the starting point of all Quaker spirituality, but listening and waiting in Meeting was and is not the end—even vocal ministry is not. The end or point of learning to listen for his voice was life in Christ. The discipline of hearing and obeying practiced in worship needed to be carried out of the Meeting for Worship into one's daily life, into one's activities in the world. Early Quakers were not contemplatives. They were simple lay men and women—married mostly, often rudely educated and active in every kind of human work. They lived in a tumultuous society at a tumultuous time in history. They traveled, preached, went to jail, challenged entrenched social customs, and tested the limits of religious orthodoxy. A generation later, a certain withdrawal from the world would become part of the Quaker way of life, but even in that more quietistic time, Friends never would withdraw from the daily routines of family, business, and ordinary human life. Also, the silence and inner stillness were never meant to bring one into any kind of contemplative state. They were meant to keep you in the life and power of Christ wherever you were.

The writings of early Friends are filled with words and phrases that evoke the waiting atmosphere of Meeting: "be still and silent," "stand single to the Lord," keep "the mind stayed upon the Lord," and others. But these phrases, which can be plucked from Quaker writings like ripe fruit, rarely refer to Meeting for Worship, but rather to the general hustle and bustle of everyday life. Life was not to be divided into an hour or two of attentiveness to God each week followed by hours and hours of preoccupation with human affairs.

Dedication to the discipline of self-denial and attention to the Spirit of Christ brought results. It transformed individual lives and it transformed the Christian life of the whole community of Quaker believers. People testified that they felt in themselves palpably passing from death to life, from spiritual bondage to Christian freedom, a resurrection of the "first Adam." Early Friends firmly believed that a life lived in the power of God's spirit did not have to remain fallen and unredeemed.

> Christ, the second Adam is come, that the dead in the first Adam might have Life, might be quickened and might be awakened to Righteousness. . . . And so, he invites all Adam's posterity to come to him, that all through him might believe, come to the Light . . . to Life, and . . . up into Peace and rest. . . .[8]

This is what I felt—profound love and the sense of being at the beginning of a journey into the depths of something utterly endless and boundless and good.

Simplicity, Integrity, and Plainness of Speech

The idea of looking solely to God for one's direction, of turning one's gaze from all the pressures and preoccupations of the "world" one was living in, led to a kind of radical simplicity about what was important in life. For me it is especially hard to tease apart the testimonies of simplicity, integrity, and plainness of speech, all testimonies of high importance to me, so I will deal with them here together. Simplicity for Friends involved a turning away from the two things human beings are most likely to worship in place of God—the self and the world. The "world" in this context is *not* the "world" of John 3:16,

> For God so loved the world, that he gave his only Son, so that everyone who believes in him may not perish but may have eternal life.

but the "world" of 1 John 2:15–16.

> Do not love the world or the things in the world. The love of the Father is not in those who love the world; for all that is in the world—the desire of the flesh, the desire of the eyes, the pride in riches—comes not from the Father but from the world.

The good "world" was the creation and the humanity made in God's image and likeness, the world that God's love "was toward" as early Friends put it. It was the world God's love went out to in spite of all the problems man's disobedience brought. The "fallen" or bad "world" was the unjust and tawdry world of things that fed human pride and sparked human lust: superfluous possessions, customs and traditions that set one person or class or race up over another, transient and unimportant things that people loved instead of loving God. As people came into a sense of God's real presence in them, however, the vanities and attractions of this "world" lost their allure:

> . . . we received the gospel with a ready mind, and with broken hearts, and affected spirits; and gave up to follow the Lord fully, casting off the weights and burdens. . . . Oh, the strippings of all needless apparel, and the forsaking of superfluities in meats, drinks, and in the plain self-denying path we walked. . . . Our words were few and savory, our apparel and houses plain, being stripped of superfluities; our countenances grave. . . . Indeed we were a plain, broken-hearted, contrite spirited, self-denying people; our souls being in an unexpressible travail to do all things well pleasing in the sight of God, for our great concern night and day was to obtain through Jesus Christ the great work of salvation, and thereby an assurance of the everlasting rest and Sabbath of our God.[9]

There was an eagerness to deny self not only by denying oneself things but by denying self-inflating impulses and expressions of every kind. Early Friends wore somber looks and refrained even from superficial conversation lest it proceed from a worldly, frivolous spirit rather than from God. They spoke slowly and with much deliberation. They avoided what we usually think of as simple distractions—games, sports, plays, and shows of all kinds because they believed that these things "trained up people to vanity and looseness, and led them from the fear of God . . ."[10]

Their suspicion of worldly customs and manners was profound, especially those that led away from the recognition of Christ's centrality, such as religious holidays or festivals that Friends thought had corrupted the church—even day and month names that retained a trace of pagan influence. Friends stopped celebrating religious holidays they considered tarnished with pagan worship such as Easter and Christmas, much as evangelical Christians today are troubled by our modern celebration of Halloween. But mostly they challenged secular customs that fed people's pride or sense of self-importance—customs of class or social order that marked one person's superiority or mastery over another. The contemporary custom of using the pronoun "you" to address social superiors and "thee" to address equals and social inferiors came under attack. Friends addressed everyone in the familiar form as a testimony against this distinction of persons. Similarly the custom of doffing one's hat to social superiors ("hat honor") or using common titles such as "Your Honor," "Your Excellency," "Your Highness," or "Sir"—even Mr. and Mrs.—all these things were abandoned by early Friends.

Modern Friends continue certain practices that flow out of these testimonies but not all. They do not, of course, celebrate Christmas or Easter in a "liturgical" way any more than they celebrate Sunday (First Day) in this way. But they do not challenge observance of the day of Christmas the way they once did, keeping their shops open. Friends are more like everyone else with respect to these holidays, trimming trees and going on Easter egg hunts with children. They do retain the use of nonpagan based names for days of the week and months of the year—calling them by their number rather than any name; but their observance of this venerable Quaker custom is formal only. The offense taken to pagan cultural remnants is no longer there. Even among Christian Friends, the offense to such small remnants seems not to have endured over the years.

The main thing with respect to the simplicity testimony that has changed over the years is the loss of any deep or radical concern about either "the self" or "the world" as early Friends understood them. Indeed, the modern infatuation with "self" (self-esteem, self-actualization, self-determination, etc.) seemed fully to have captured Friends by the 1980s as it had captured most Americans. There is little sense among modern Friends that the self needs to turn from death to life or from "fall" to "restoration." The only really negative talk you hear of "the world" is the world of capitalist enterprise—the materialism promoted by Madison Avenue, the manipulations of industrialists or manufacturers, or Big Money. In this, modern Friends are virtually indistinguishable from politically left-wing critics of American business. The world is never the things that *we* are part of, that *we* are tempted by. As Fox once wrote, the problem is always "they," "they," "they," never "I," "I," "I."

The reduction of spiritual issues to political or social ones was deeply bothersome to me, as I have said several times. It sapped the faith of any real need for Christ and failed to recognize that the deepest barriers in us that kept us from God were not societal but spiritual. I already lived my life wary of the kind of materialism capitalism promoted. Simplicity for me involved more things like avoiding political or philosophical fads, trying not to be overly cerebral about what I believed, speaking what was on my mind and heart simply and directly and trying not to be manipulative or devious in my dealings with others. These were the parts of the simplicity testimony that came to mean most to me, maybe because talking and arguing about ideologies was something I had done a lot.

If you believe that God dwells in you and works in and through you, then it is your responsibility to treat your words and acts with respect by making sure that what you say and do comes as much as is possible from a sprit of love, that it is sincere, and that it comes from a deeper place in you than off the top of your head. How what you say or do is received or whether it changes anything is not for you to worry about. Examples of the kind of speech I am talking about are very common, such as words of apology or repentance for things you have said or done in anger or impatience. If, like me, you lose your temper with people in frustrating circumstances—you are forced to stand in line endlessly or have to deal with people who cannot understand some important, complex issue you need to work out with them—if the Lord puts a word of repentance in you to offer to that offended party, you have an obligation to act on it. It doesn't matter that it was a week or two weeks ago. It doesn't matter that you might go through the rest of your life without ever having to cross paths with that person again, you have an obligation to go back and try to apologize.

Or perhaps you have a family member or friend with whom you have long-standing and intractable "issues." In these situations too, you have a duty to speak thoughtfully, lovingly, and with integrity what the Lord gives you to say. I know I did. There were family members who had hurt me many times over the years, relationships that were tortured and difficult because my need for them had always been so great. People who come from broken, dysfunctional families like mine will easily be able to understand what I am talking about even without the boring details. There was a need and a call in me to "speak truth" in love to members of my family and also, for the first time, an ability to accept the broken reality I had always previously hoped would be healed by my silence or endurance. I could not cure things in my own will. Perhaps it would not be God's will either that everything be cured the way I had in mind. But my job was not the end result. My job was only to be faithful to the little truths I believed God had given me to speak.

At the time of my convincement I had many calls to this type of ministry of simple and direct words: testifying to my faith, speaking truth to family members and friends, speaking in Meeting, speaking words of repentance. I had a vivid dream in which God was caused pain because I would not speak a word to my sister about my new faith in him. She experienced her first really psychotic breakdown shortly after returning to New York from the visit with me I have described, where we looked for clues as to my son's whereabouts. She was once again in the hopsital. I could not put the dream out of my mind. It was like the times I had had Eliot's words on my mind in Meeting years before. But my sister was not in any kind of shape to hear such words or respond to them. I knew in my heart it would be useless, maybe even provocative to her to bring up something as controversial as religion. But God would not let me not speak. So

I did on one visit—uncomfortably and inarticulately—and I wrote her to follow up. I wish I could tell you a miracle came from it, but it didn't. I cannot know everything about it; I only know it had to be done. I would not have been faithful had I not spoken.

These were the kinds of messy but nonetheless compelling "speaking" matters I felt called to in the early days of my conversion, things I saw as part of the call to simplicity—simple responsiveness to God's will in the small things of my life. Some resulted in good; some resulted in ambiguous outcomes. I mention them because they seemed to me the arena in which my faith was called to work. The rewards I experienced from faithfulness in these small things were very great though, greater than I can describe.

The other virtue closely connected with simplicity for early Friends was the call to integrity. When they stood before a magistrate, they refused to make a ceremony of honesty by employing oaths. They simply kept to "yes" and "no" as Jesus had urged (Matt. 5:37). Fox and other leaders continually stressed the importance of integrity as part of the witness they made:

> Do rightly, justly, truly, holily, equally to all people in all things. . . .
>
> Wrong no man, over-reach no man, if it be never so much to your advantage, but be plain, righteous and holy. . . . Let justice be acted and holiness in all things, without any guile, fraud or deceit. . . .
>
> Loathe deceit . . . hard-heartedness, wronging, cozening, cheating or unjust dealing. But live and reign in the righteous Life and Power of God . . . doing the Truth to all, without respect to persons, high or low whatsoever, young or old, rich or poor . . .
>
> . . . live in the Power of Truth and Wisdom of God, to answer the just Principle of God in all people upon the earth. And so answering . . . it, thereby you come to be as a city set upon a hill. . . . So, let your lives preach, let your Light shine, that your works may be seen, your Father may be glorified, your fruits may be unto holiness and that your end may be everlasting Life. . . .[11]

Friends' reputation for honesty and fair dealing became legendary and remains a source of justifiable pride among Friends. Honesty had always been something important to me, but now I fully recognized and acknowledged God's part in that in my life.

Equality of Persons

Early Friends' testimony on the equality and worth of all men and women is another fruit of Friends' faith from the beginning. But again the basis of this testimony has shifted over the years. Early Friends saw the equality of the sexes as something that flowed from the "restoration" Christ had brought to pass on earth. God had never intended men and women to be unequal (Gen. 1:26–27 and Gen. 2:18). The subordination of women to men had arisen in the fall (Gen. 3:16); but with the fall overcome in Christ, the subordination of women was meant to cease.

> . . . man and woman were meet-helps [companions and helpers to one another] (before they fell) and the image of God and righteousness and holiness; and so they are to be again in the restoration by Christ Jesus.[12]

The restoration came with Christ, with the institution of the new covenant and the outpouring of his Spirit that had come at Pentecost. Again, Fox pointed to Peter's first address to the people of Jerusalem, a speech I have already quoted in my discussion of early Friends' theology. Christ's coming was the fulfillment of Joel's prophecy that God's Spirit would be poured out on all flesh. "Your sons and your daughters shall prophesy. . . . Even upon my slaves, both men and women, in those days I will pour out my Spirit; and they shall prophesy" (Acts 2:17–18). As women converts came into the life and power of Christ as Friends, they too began to preach and prophesy. Fox defended them in an England that saw this as an affront to proper church order. As to the admonitions against women preaching in Paul's letter to Timothy (1 Tim. 2:12), Fox developed complex arguments to reconcile his views. He never doubted that women had a right and a duty to respond to Christ's call in them to preach, teach, or prophesy. Women played a vital role in the building of the early Quaker movement. Many preached and some even traveled to the far ends of the earth to proclaim the gospel Friends were preaching. One woman, Mary Dyer, died as a martyr for responding to that call—hanged by the Puritans of Massachusetts in 1660 along with three Quaker men called to the same ministry.

It was this same sense of what life "in the restoration by Christ Jesus" was to be that shaped the Friends' wedding ceremony. Just as God had joined Adam and Eve together without the mediation of any other human being, so Friends too believed it should be among them. Friends who desired to marry were not joined by any minister or officiating elder or clerk of the Meeting. They simply met in a Meeting for Worship and stood in the group to exchange their promises to love and care for the other, "with divine assistance."

The question of racial equality did not really confront Friends until they began to travel to those parts of the world where slavery was practiced. While Fox made it clear that Friends who were slave owners should exercise kindness and teach their slaves the gospel, he clung to the biblical letter here and did not see slavery as a fundamental offense against the gospel of Christ. John Woolman, in eighteenth-century America, would be the one to lead Friends to the insight that any participation in the institution of slavery was inconsistent with Christian practice.

Modern Friends found early Friends' testimonies about sex and race very meaningful, but not for the same reasons. Modern Friends' testimony is based much more on the values and principles of the Enlightenment than on any principle early Friends articulated. The problem with that did not become entirely clear to me until some years later when I thought through some of the dilemmas modern feminism was causing us in the Society.

Peace

The final testimony of early Friends that has had lasting value to Friends is the peace testimony. The peace testimony was not clearly enunciated by Friends until 1660. There is even some evidence that Fox may have believed in the 1650s that Oliver Cromwell's army would have a role to play in the end-time scenario he believed his reproclamation of the "true gospel" might inaugurate in England.[13] Much of Fox's most successful evangelization in the 1650s was among the soldiery of this army. This may have even been true, though he made it quite clear that he personally felt from the start that he had been called into "the virtue of that life and power that took away the occasion of all wars. . . ."[14]

By 1660, however, Fox had become clearer on the matter. He and eleven other Quaker leaders issued a statement at that time that soon became official policy for all Friends:

> We know that wars and fightings proceed from the lusts of men (as Jas. iv. 1-3), out of which lusts the Lord hath redeemed us, and so out of the occasion of war. [. . .] All bloody principles and practices, we, as to our own particulars, do utterly deny, with all outward wars and strife and fightings with outward weapons, for any end or under any pretence whatsoever. And this is our testimony to the whole world.
>
> [. . .] the spirit of Christ, by which we are guided, is not changeable, so as once to command us from a thing as evil and again to move unto it; and we do certainly know, and so testify to the world, that the spirit of Christ, which leads us into all Truth, will never move us to fight and war against any man with outward weapons, neither for the kingdom of Christ, nor for the kingdoms of this world.[15]

The testimonies I have touched on in this chapter were not the only ones. In the nineteenth century, Friends made it a very clear testimony to avoid the use of alcohol and, later, drugs. They also frowned on gambling or toying with "chance" or "luck" in any way. They adopted a testimony against the use of capital punishment. But the bottom line for early Friends was the idea of hearing and obeying—being singularly attentive to the light and word of Christ in you and doing what he commanded with undivided heart, even if it meant embracing the cross. The cross, as I have said, was central to Friends.

> Where the world is standing the Cross is not lived in. But dwelling in the Cross to the world, here the Love of God is shed abroad in

the heart and the Way is opened in the inheritance, which fades not away. . .[16]

The Prophetic Dimension of Friends' Spirituality

The fact that Friends saw themselves as responding to God's living voice within made them see themselves in some measure as prophets of his word to the world. Hearing and obeying the word of God was the occupation of a prophet. You may not be called to go out and do some great and memorable deed, but you were called to do what God led you to do even if it involved risks. Mary Fisher, a simple English housemaid, believed God was calling her to witness the gospel to the Sultan of Turkey, who ruled over an empire that posed a military threat to Europe in the seventeenth century. She traveled many months to obey this call and even managed to get an audience with him. I have mentioned the Friends who died obeying a call they believed they had from God to witness against the Puritans' prohibition against the free circulation of Quaker tracts in New England. This prophetic dimension of Friends early witness is sometimes overlooked in presentations of Friends' testimonies and spirituality. But I mention it because it played a role in my journey from the beginning, whether I felt called to speak in vocal ministry or in other more worldly contexts or at the end when I felt called to leave and return to the Catholic Church. The sense of being in the same place in relation to God as the prophets has always been something I felt as a Friend.

Modern Friends are much less reticent talking about the testimonies Friends hold than they are about what Friends believe theologically. Many people, like me, were drawn to Friends precisely for these testimonies, especially the peace testimony, so I experienced the difference in what it was to see those testimonies prior to becoming Christian and after my convincement. The antiwar movement of the sixties attracted many people to the pacifist views of Quakerism. The track record of the Society—being so early an opponent of slavery, recognizing the humanity of the American Indian tribes they settled near, providing leadership to the women's suffrage movement, and other progressive stances they have taken over the years—these things were very appealing to many of us who grew up believing in the struggle for civil rights for blacks and then for women, fighting against the war in Vietnam, and struggling to bring about a society we thought would be more just. The environmental movement of the seventies and eighties also found values and commitment in Friends' testimonies that supported their concerns with the idea of stewardship over the creation. So many of the movements of the post World War II era found resonance in the traditions and values of Friends. The problem was that without a strong foundation and articulation of the theological roots of all these testimonies, the modern Society tended to adopt the secular reasoning and language of the wider movements. Quaker "guides" or disciplines[17] tended to hold onto older quotations and references back to early Friends beliefs, but the common parlance and logic of Friends on these issues was hardly distinguishable from that of the antiestablishment groups that existed outside Friends. What is missing from the modern way of understanding and articulating Friends' testimonies is any kind of radical call to holiness especially in relation to personal, sexual behavior. And there is no room for the call to lowliness or self-abnegation; there is little comfort with the sense of sin early Quakers found so important in coming into the sense of God's new covenant presence. But it is in the discernment process (or lack of one) that one really sees what modernism has wrought among Friends.

8

Continuing Revelation, Discernment, and Modern Friends

Now I come to what many who admire Friends' spirituality see as the "fly in the ointment." How can you be sure that the voice you are hearing and obeying is God's voice? This was the question that my friend (later my husband) was seeking an answer to in joining the Society of Friends. It was no trouble in the 1970s and '80s to find support for the idea—revolutionary in the seventeenth century—that the individual might come into a personal sense of what truth is. Everyone I knew in the 1970s and '80s believed that he or she could arrive at truth through his or her own efforts—trial, error, reflection, consultation with others. The really tough question was how could you know if your view of the truth was true. Was anything really true in an absolute sense? When I met him, my friend was wondering about these things and exploring the possibility that the religious traditions of Judaism and Christianity—the wisdom and experience reflected in the Scriptures—might be some guide to his own personal efforts in this regard.

The religious vision of early Friends held a lot of appeal to people raised on the kind of mindset I have described. Fox's conviction that the inward Teacher would direct all people without the need for others to instruct them, the sense he had of Scripture being secondary to the Spirit in terms of authority, his call for people to come away from the dry husks of outward forms and legalism in religion all seemed consistent with the notion that individuals could find their way on their own.

Contemporaries of Fox often mocked the Friends' assertion that they could know God's will experientially without the aid of church authority or Scripture. Fox tells of one incident he faced:

> [. . .] one [man] burst out into a passion and said he could speak his experiences as well as I; but I told him experience was one thing but to go with a message and a word from the Lord as the prophets and the apostles had and did, and as I had done to them, this was another thing.[1]

Fox did not think he was promoting religious subjectivism. He really thought it was Christ—the Christ of the Scriptures and the Christ of history—who dwelled in us and taught us the way to go. But this Spirit of Christ and the truths he embodied were not reducible to church formulas or dead and encased in Scripture texts. This Christ lived. He was resurrected and with us always. Fox and early Friends very much believed in the reality of God's continuing revelation in history.

One of the best vehicles modern Friends used to get across the Quaker idea of continuing revelation was a story George Fox's wife told in her introduction to the 1694 edition of Fox's journal. Margaret Fell Fox and her first husband, a prominent judge, lived on a large estate in northwest England, Swarthmore Hall. The Fells were known for the hospitality they typically extended to traveling preachers of all kinds, so Fox and a friend of his stopped by and met the lady of the house. Judge Fell was away. Margaret Fell went to hear Fox preach at her local church and was moved by his plea that people needed to experience Christ in their own lives and not rely so exclusively on the Scriptures or others' interpretation of Scripture to define the truth about Christ. She recorded the words Fox addressed to the congretation:

> "You will say, Christ saith this, and the apostles say this; but what canst thou say? Art thou a child of Light and hast walked in the Light, and what thou speakest is it inwardly from God?"

> This opened me so that it cut me to the heart; and then I saw clearly we were all wrong. So I sat me down in my pew again, and cried bitterly. And I cried in my spirit to the Lord, "We are all thieves, we are all thieves, we have taken the Scripture in words and know nothing of them in ourselves."[2]

The truths contained in the Scriptures were truths that we could know in immediate and personal terms. They were truths we could embody in words of our own. God was alive and guiding men and women today just as he had guided them in Moses' time, in the prophets' time and in Jesus' time. It was one thing to recognize the Scriptures as authentically recording the words and truths opened to godly men and women in former times, but it was quite another to deny that God could speak in and through people in other times and places.

God's revelation cannot be limited to a prescribed form of words, whether scriptural or credal; it continues and sometimes even changes as our understanding of God's will evolves. The example most often given of this is the change that occurred when Friends in the eighteenth century decided that slave holding was inconsistent with Christian profession and would henceforth be prohibited for members of the Society of Friends. God did do new things in history—not contradictory things, but things that revealed the underlying order and coherence of his will. It is clear from reading the Scriptures that there was a time in history when the holding of slaves or participation in slavery systems was not understood by even holy men and women as being fundamentally inconsistent with God's redemptive plan. But such an understanding did come to pass, and Friends were among the first to grasp it.

The idea of "continuing revelation" was a very important concept for early Friends, but it didn't stand alone. It stood in tension with another important idea—the idea that the Spirit of God that brought forth all truth was not a God of disorder. The best articulation of this in the early years was in Robert Barclay's *Apology*, published first in 1673 to defend Friends' interpretation of the gospel against charges of heresy. Barclay defends the idea that the Spirit of God continues to lead and influence the faithful, but he is careful to assure his readers that such continuing revelation will never lead to utterly new and contradictory "truths."

> We firmly believe that there is no other doctrine or gospel to be preached other than that which was delivered by the apostles. And we freely subscribe to the saying in Gal 1:8: "If we or an angel from heaven should proclaim to you a gospel contrary to what we proclaimed to you, let that one be accursed."
>
> In other words, we distinguish between a revelation of a new gospel and new doctrines, and new insight into the established gospel and doctrines. We plead for the latter, but we utterly deny the former. We firmly believe that there are no new foundations to be laid other than those which have already been laid. But added insight is needed on matters for which the foundations have already been laid.[3]

Early Friends knew that there were competing voices within people, and they knew and spoke eloquently about the fact that hearing and obeying God required a personal experience of Christ's cross in relation to their own wills and selves. Fox himself had struggled against the competing voices that called to him, the "two thirsts" that clamored within him for attention during Christ's ministration to him in the "spiritual wilderness" (the "ministration of Moses" in his own journey). When certain early recruits to the Quaker vision of the gospel went off on escapades Fox thought were not authentic or that brought the movement into disrepute, he set up a structure of Monthly Meetings that he hoped would oversee individuals and test their leadings. But I don't think Fox ever fully appreciated the potential for confusion that lay in his rejection of outward standards. He simply believed that the gospel he had recovered had a power and an order in it that reached to the heart and transformed it. Christ's sheep "'know his voice. They will not follow a stranger, but they will run from him because they do not know the voice of strangers'" (John 10:4–5). If there were disorderly people in a Monthly Meeting, he encouraged the "more seasoned" to go to them and labor with them as Jesus recommends in Matthew's gospel (18:15–17).

Still, there were some outward guideposts or principles you could employ in discernment. These were never written in the form of rules (heaven forbid!); they simply developed over time.

One was insisting on the unchanging nature of God's truth. Just as the promises of Christ are utterly constant, so the "spirit of Christ, by which we are guided, is not changeable, so as once to command us from a thing as evil and again to move unto it; . . ."[4] This principle was associated with Friends' articulation of their peace testimony, but it was equally applicable to all the truths they saw as flowing from God.

Also, the Spirit of Christ they had "come into" was the same Spirit that had "given forth" the Scriptures, so it stood to reason that Scripture could be used to test the consistency of one's personal leading to the witness of Christ contained there. The fruits of your profession should be fruits of the Spirit—"love, joy, peace, patience, kindness, generosity, faithfulness, gentleness and self-control"(Gal. 5:22)—not the fruits of the "fleshly," unredeemed nature—"fornication, impurity . . . idolatry. . . strife, jealousy, anger, . . . and things like these" (Gal. 5:19–21). Or, if there was a clear statement of principle set forth there, you could not easily set yourself in opposition to it. Friends denied that this amounted to "setting up" Scripture as an outward authority, but the effect was much the same. If Scripture clearly testified to something and you felt led to a path that was inconsistent with it, or if the fruits of what you believed promised to be bad or destructive, you were likely to be judged out of unity with the Truth.

Yet there are difficulties. The Scriptures, if viewed as a matter of words only, contain inconsistent admonitions. On the question of slavery, for example, there are words that seem to sanction or accept slavery as a part of civilized life, which believers may participate in—such as Paul's advice to slaves to "obey [their] earthly masters with fear and trembling, in singleness of heart, as you obey Christ . . ." (Eph. 6:5). Yet Friends challenged the definitiveness of Paul's words in several ways—by examining closely the "fruits" of slavery in both slaveowner and slave and finding them universally corrupting and destructive, and second, by arguing that the whole tenor and development of the biblical "story" that God's Spirit had given forth that man was not to be viewed or used as chattel.

Christ was the same yesterday, today, and tomorrow as far as Friends were concerned. Another way of applying the test of consistency was to ask if the Christ you were listening to and obeying inwardly was the same Christ that the Scriptures had revealed, or if he had changed to suit the times you lived in. This standard was beautifully articulated by James Nayler:

> Now seeing he has appeared who is from everlasting and changes not, here is an everlasting trial for you all [. . .] whether you profess him from the letter or the light; come try [test] whether Christ is in you. Measure your life and weigh your profession with that which cannot deceive you, which has stood and will stand forever, for he is sealed of the father.
>
> First, see if your Christ be the same that was from everlasting to everlasting, or is he changed according to the times: [. . .] Does he whom you obey as your leader lead you out to war against this world and all the pride and glory, fashions and customs, love and pleasures, and whatever else is not of God therein? Does he justify any life now but what he justified in the prophets and apostles and saints of old?[5]

Were you led into the same kind of lowliness Christ exemplified, or were you led into self-aggrandizement and pride, thinking you knew more than you really did? Did you seek to justify a way of life that was fundamentally different from the way of life the saints had always been called to live or to seek some liberty no follower of Christ would have sought? The standard was not changed—only the means by which we came into a knowledge of that standard.

Were you eager to serve others and to shed the love of God abroad, or were you led into actions that served your own interests?

> [. . .] be servants to the Truth and do not strive for mastery, but serve one another in Love, "Wash one another's feet" (John 13:14). Take Christ for your example that I may hear of no strife among you.[6]

Were you enamored of worldly fashions and honors, or did you turn your back on these things as Christ had? Infatuation with the world's delights had to be put aside if one was to come into the life Christ offered, for that life lay on the other side of his cross.

The idea of checking one's own sense of who Christ was with the Christ of Scripture was an important one to me. I remember wondering how modern Friends could be so cavalier about not feeling they needed be familiar with the Scriptures, when really the only way we could be introduced to Christ was through these early writings. That he was more than the writings, I could accept; but that he could be known without first being revealed to us through the men who had known him or known others who had known him—this I had trouble seeing. The Scriptures were not dispensable even if they were not completely exhaustive.

The other part of the Friends' discernment approach that I found meaningful was the way they used the idea of the cross—that the life Christ offered us was on the other side of the cross. The way this worked was simple—you could test a leading by asking yourself if the leading would bring you satisfaction and a sense of fulfilled desire or restraint and self-denial. If the leading served your "worldly desires" or gratified you in some immediate way, it was probably not from God. I know this sounds crazy to modern ears, perhaps a little masochistic too. But it was not. Maybe it was oversimplified, but the idea of it was that if something you felt called to do simply served you, your wishes, or your will, it probably was something rooted in your own will. And what you strove to come into as a Friend was to stand in God's will and come into a life that stood in his will. The testimony of Friends was that this life would ultimately be much richer and much better than any life you could conceive of in your own power.

If I wanted my friend to give up on his marriage and divorce his wife so we could marry, that desire had to go to the cross as much as I could let it. If I wanted to leave town so I could get a completely new start and find a job that paid real money, that too had to go to the cross. If I did things out of a desire for recognition or praise or reward of any kind, that too was suspect under this stringent test. It wasn't that any of these things was necessarily bad. It was just that they stood in my own will. Things that came from God were "bestowed," not seized. The life that is really life for human beings is the life that comes after the cross is accepted.

Another important principle of discernment among Friends was the principle of testing individual leadings against the corporate judgment of the gathered Meeting. This was the whole purpose of what later came to be called the Meeting for Business. Here "clearness" could be sought by individuals who felt burdened with some "leading" or "call" they needed support for—like traveling in the ministry or undertaking some project requiring resources beyond those personally available. The Meeting could also step in if it was united in believing that a Friend had overstepped his or her guide or brought disrepute on the Society.

The principles outlined here created among Friends a conservative way of containing the dangers inherent in their new covenant approach to Christ's gospel. And when they were combined with the system Friends developed for conducting business and making changes in the established decisions and conducting the practical affairs of the Society, they were very stable indeed. Indeed, it was difficult to make any changes to established ways of conducting community business or articulating the principles of the Society. Any policy or practice formally instituted by a Meeting or Yearly Meeting for its constitutive Meetings was impossible to change without there being "unity" to change it—and unity meant fundamental accord among everyone involved in the business session called to consider the policy. There were a few ways around this demand, but very few. It would be too complicated to describe in detail the business procedures Friends instituted in the early days of the Society, but they have kept the Society's formal documents (the minutes and disciplines published by Meetings and Yearly Meetings) very "traditional," very consistent with early documents and statements.

Yet the statements themselves are not technically binding, and the way things are articulated outside the documents, among members, tends to stray a good deal from official statements—adopting contemporary ideas, approaches, and ways of articulating values. The whole tenor of antiwar discussions among Friends during the Vietnam conflict varied hardly a whit from what I had heard among atheistic antiwar activists. Of course, I speak only from my own experience here and do not mean to imply that Friends elsewhere did not employ more faith-based rationales for opposing the war. But I also noticed this in other areas as well, such as support for women's rights and human rights generally. Here Friends' articulation was rooted in Enlightenment rights theory—not in any radical understanding of Christ's teaching.

In the early 1980s, when I was considering joining Friends, the issues of continuing revelation and the question of personal and community discernment were at the root of many of the tensions that existed in the Society. There was no unity among unprogrammed Friends on the question of whether or not the Scriptures were texts somehow "given forth" by the Spirit we worshipped, and there was no fundamental unity over the nature or identity of that Spirit itself. So while most Friends went about confidently asserting that the Spirit was giving forth truth today as it had done throughout history, virtually every attempt to test openings against Scripture or against tradition fell flat. In the year when I was considering joining, however, the seriousness of the situation did not hit me. It seemed so logically possible to win the day—everything in the earliest witness of Friends was so consistent and so deeply Christian it just seemed impossible for things to be as off track as they now sometimes appeared. But time would change my assessment.

The year I took to explore Friends' history and thought also involved getting more involved with things on the local level. I explored other Friends' organizations and gatherings. I got involved with the First Day School program at my Meeting, teaching the group of boys who were my son's age, attended the business meetings that took place every month, and took a greater interest in the issues and activities the Meeting was involved in. I also went to our Yearly Meeting and a large summer gathering of liberal unprogrammed meetings from the east coast of the United States called Friends General Conference. FGC was a large weeklong gathering of Friends that took place on a college campus every year. Over the next few years I would attend FGC gatherings at Ithaca, New York; Slippery Rock, Pennsylvania; Berea, Kentucky; and at St. Lawrence College in upstate New York. There were speakers and workshops, worship-sharing groups, and informal gatherings of people with shared concerns for any number of different things. I was not yet a member of the Religious Society of Friends when I started attending these gatherings, but I was considering joining and it seemed a good way to get to know the group better. Friends are part of a network of wider fellowships that radiate out from their local Meetings or worship groups. The tensions roiling Quakerism during the years I am describing were especially noticeable at the FGC gatherings—the tension between more traditionally Christian Friends and universalist or even nontheistic Friends, along with the tensions raised by the impact of the sexual revolution that was taking place everywhere in American in the seventies and eighties—feminism, homosexuality, dissatisfaction with traditional ideas about marriage, etc. The Christian-Universalist dialogue was the one I was most involved with during my first years among Friends.

As part of our effort to advance the Christian reform movement we hoped would gain momentum in the Society, my friend and I offered workshops and worship groups at both the Yearly Meeting gathering, which took place in Tennessee, and at the FGC gathering as well. Like many Christian Friends during this period, we tried to find ways of bringing the message to Friends and giving support to Christian Friends who wanted to see Quakerism keep alive the theological foundations and traditions of early Friends.

That spring of 1980, we also worked to put together a set of quotations from the Scriptures and from Friends' writings over the three hundred years of their history to show the unequivocally Christian character of those writings. The Yearly Meeting (Southern Appalachian Yearly Meeting and Association [SAYMA]) was engaged in a revision of its *Faith and Practice,* and I think we were hoping that the quotes might find a way into the revised guide or at least be used as a resource.

At Friends General Conference that summer, I observed the most liberal face of American Quakerism. What I remember the most was the huge influence feminist thought and critique was having on Friends. I knew one of the reasons the Yearly Meeting guide was being revised had to do with a desire Friends had to make the language of it more inclusive. This was a common complaint about language from feminists during this time, and Friends sought to remedy it in their own publications. One of the main speakers at the FGC gathering was a feminist who called into question the justice of giving any authority to tradition when that tradition arose from societies that had been patriarchal and somehow by definition oppressive to women. The voice of women could not be found in traditions that predated modern feminism, and God should not be thought of as Father. The language that we used for God had to change. It excluded women and made them feel second rate. The tenor of the speech disturbed me and put me off, but it would be years before I put together a coherent response. For the present, all I knew was that what she claimed was not my experience of the tradition. I had not felt at all excluded or oppressed by the tradition I had come to understand. Quite the contrary—the tradition in its seventeenth-century form had brought me to life, but everywhere it was coming under attack.

The situation didn't seem entirely bleak, however. Many people at these conferences were also responsive to the message of early Friends, which individual Christian Friends and groups like New Foundation put before Friends in different ways. The number of Christian Friends seemed to me to be growing, and they were young and charismatic and full of optimism about the power of the gospel to transform people and groups.

After a little more than a year, I made the decision to join the Society of Friends. It was not a decision that implied complete accord or comfort with the state of things among Friends, or even complete agreement with everything early Friends had said about the gospel. I was not entirely in agreement with early Friends' radical rejection of outward things. To me it seemed obvious that the outward dimension of our human lives—our experiences, words, histories, etc.—played an essential role in the "epistemology" of faith, its development in us. We needed to get to know the Christ who was in us by getting acquainted with him in the Scriptures, and we came to know him better if we understood the ways he brought to fulfillment so many of the "types and shadows" that embodied God's presence under the old covenant. My whole journey had been one of coming to know *within* the things I had stumbled around outwardly for years. I could in no way say from my experience that I could have come into these things without the outward dimension, but I didn't hold Fox's rejection of "outwardness" against him either. I just sensed that what he had meant by "outward" was different in some essential way from what modern people understood by the term. Modern Friends had a much more rigorous sense of what was to be understood by "outward," including in the concept not only outward rites or formulas but even the concepts embodied in the words we used, the conceptual and linguistic forms the Christian religion had taken in its development.

The other thing I could not accept was early Friends' complete rejection of sixteen hundred years of church history as sunk in apostasy. This seemed to me a little over the top, part of the Reformation's radical rejection of the "tradition" as it had developed in the Catholic Church. But I excused these excesses by seeing Friends to some extent as prophets to the churches of the seventeenth century. They had not recovered a lost gospel; they had simply challenged Christians in all churches against getting caught up in the outward forms of Christianity—whether the outward form was a way of worshipping, a credal formula, or a way of approaching Scripture—and to emphasize the inward and experiential dimension of the gospel in which they professed to believe. Then again, I tried to look past this disagreement by not seeing it as something central to the early Quaker message but something incidental only, a part of their Reformation zeal.

More troubling to me at the time than these apparently minor imperfections in seventeenth-century Quaker thought was the spiritual condition of the modern Society of Friends. But, as I've said, it seemed to me that there was reason to be hopeful. There was a lot of energy in the reform movement, and many good people committed to it. And the truth was, even those Friends I disagreed with fundamentally I thought of as thoughtful and spiritually earnest people. I liked them and admired them for the sincerity with which they approached questions of religious truth. I had been a doubter for years. Who was I to expect everyone around me to see what it had taken me so long to see? It was a good place for a doubter to become a believer.

Did I think about going back to the Catholic Church at any time? Yes, I did, but not deeply or seriously. I had not left the Catholic Church for any reason that had to do with it in itself. No one in the Church had ever disappointed me or oppressed me in any of the ways in which I had so often heard ex-Catholics complain. I had no complaint against the Church at all. On the contrary, I loved the Church and all that I had experienced of it, and in a mysterious way, I think I still felt a kind of indelibility in the seal that my baptism there had placed on me, but these things did not seem compelling to me at the time. The gospel of early Friends was what had reached me when I was beyond reach, and I felt a sense of commitment to that gospel. I loved the Meeting for Worship and the sense of personal relationship to God and expectancy I felt there—that God might use me in some way to point to his reality, to speak his invitation to others, to live in his will.

I submitted a letter of application and asked for a "clearness committee" to be formed to review it and talk to me. A group of four to six people were asked by the Meeting clerk to meet with me to see that I understood what I was getting into, to see if I was "clear."

The committee met once or twice with me. The issue of my marriage, now dissolved, was raised and resolved to their satisfaction. It had not been a marriage undertaken in the context of any religion, much less under the care of any Friends' Meeting—not that Friends would have refused me membership had it been. But Friends were careful in wanting to know the status of commitments undertaken in any context. In a few months, the committee reported back to a full business session and my membership was approved. My children were also accepted into membership. They were then five and eight years old. There was very little difference between being an attender and being a member of a Meeting. The only thing membership gave me that simple attendance did not was the right to be on more committees. I was eager to be part of everything.

One of the first things I volunteered to do was join those members of Meeting who were working on the Yearly Meeting guide, but we would not be in North Carolina long enough for me to meet with the group more than once. Mostly things just went along as they had for a year. There were more SAYMA gatherings, more FGCs to attend, more New Foundation Meetings, and other Christian gatherings. Being an active Friend means being very involved in all the workings of the organization, in the lives of Friends from widely different places and Meetings, and in all the issues everyone is dealing with. In the '80s, those issues had to an extraordinary degree to do with sex and gender.

To a certain extent the issue of sexuality had been much with my friend and me from the very start. We felt like we had declared our independence from the sexual revolution in sorting through the relationship we were free to have in the first years we knew each other. We knew firsthand the emptiness of that particular revolution and knew also some of the rewards that could come from sticking to the old rules. We had struggled with restraint at times and probably cursed the rules at times, but the sense of faithfulness we derived from obeying what we thought Christ wanted for us far outweighed the fleeting frustrations we sometimes felt.

Life seemed good to me finally. My children were happy and well adjusted. The new law office I had opened rather than flitting off to a higher paying job in Baltimore was keeping me fairly busy. My ex-husband was far away through his own choice, so the tensions there had diminished. My friend's life was also getting back to normal after being full of uncertainty for so long. His wife filed for divorce and let him know there was no going back. In 1982, nearly three years after we met, "way opened," as Friends are fond of saying, for us to consider marriage. We turned again to the "clearness" process of Friends to work through issues that still hung over us, including whether or not we were free to remarry under the care of the Meeting, how we intended to deal with the remaining hostile feelings my ex-husband had toward me, and how we would approach the matter with the children. It was a good process. There were some very seasoned and wonderful Friends on our committee who understood our worries and concerns.

In May of 1982, a Meeting was held for the purpose of witnessing our marriage. It was a wonderful event. Even my father was there. He liked the silence of Meeting. Peace and quiet are things even an atheist can appreciate, and it certainly made me happy to have him—he had been at so few of the special events in my life. There were about a hundred people present. The Meeting started as usual in perfect silence; then after a period of ten to fifteen minutes we stood up and exchanged our promises—to be loving and faithful to each other with divine assistance for as long as we should live. It was the essence of simplicity. Then others were given time to reflect and to speak, as God (or whatever spirit they imagined) moved them. At the end, everyone signed a large certificate; everyone was equally a witness—young and old, male and female, Friend and non-Friend, Christian and non-Christian alike.

About a year later, we moved to New York. I gave up the practice of law and followed my husband's opportunity to teach in a Quaker school in New York, just east of the place where I had grown up. Once again I experienced a move as a kind of new beginning.

9

New York

The new home we moved to in the summer of 1983 was on Long Island, on the grounds of a well-established and prestigious Friends school where my husband had been offered a job teaching high school history and religion. The Monthly Meeting we joined was across the road from the school. The school used the Meeting House there for its weekly Meetings, but there was also a regular Monthly Meeting there on First Days. Unlike the Meeting we had belonged to in North Carolina, this Meeting was old and housed in a very historic and lovely Meeting House. Constructed in 1725, it was on the U.S. Register of Historic Buildings. The Meeting's tiny core of long-term members were descended from some of Long Island's oldest and most venerable Quaker families—the Hickses, the Scudders, the Cockses, and the Willettses—names one saw on street signs around the county. They were lovely people, but there were very few of them left and you couldn't help but realize that the thing they represented—the old guard Quaker remnant on Long Island—would soon be gone forever. There were a few newer families who were members, but a good many of the people who attended Meeting there were not Quakers. They were connected with the school in some way—people who had no other religious affiliation and who admired the values Friends stood for.

The Meeting was much more conservative politically, socially, and theologically than the Meeting we had left in North Carolina—not necessarily in the manner of seventeenth-century Friends, just conventionally more orthodox. The thing they cared most about was preserving the Meeting—its ways of doing business and conducting worship, its Meeting House, and its financial viability. They had little if any contact with wider Friends' organizations (Quarterly Meeting, Yearly Meeting, FGC, etc.) and seemed to desire little. Business Meetings tended to be taken up with maintenance of the building and grounds, for which members had a strong sense of stewardship. Individuals interested in "causes" (political, social, or charitable) were encouraged to invest whatever time and/or money they wished to in these, but the Meeting shied away from supporting such things corporately. There were in this Meeting a few universalist or nontheistic members, but they coexisted peacefully with Christian members. Vocal prayer and references to Jesus were common and did not rouse the defensiveness and disquiet they often did in other Meetings. I appreciated the peace that existed in this Meeting, even if there wasn't much fervor or energy.

The New York Yearly Meeting was another story. More than the Yearly Meeting we had left, the New York Yearly Meeting was a place where the culture wars of the post-'60s years were in full swing. "New Age" approaches to spirituality and "neo-pagan" impulses proliferated in a way I thought amazing given how pagan-phobic early Quakers had been. Support for "abortion rights" was *in* despite Friends' historic peace testimony and horror of violence generally. Sexual activists of every stripe found a hearing for making changes in the traditional sexual testimonies of Friends—historically as "puritanical" as any you could find. Feminists railed at the tyranny of traditional marriage, bisexuals and gays agitated for recognition and support for the view that Friends should be free to engage in whatever sexual practices seemed right to them regardless of biblical strictures or traditional testimonies, and universalist Friends pushed for greater recognition of their claim that Friends' spirituality, while rooted in Christianity, was no longer necessarily Christian. I had anticipated that these issues and movements would be at least as contentious in New York as they had been in SAYMA, but I had not anticipated how stressful and enervating I would find them over time.

It was no surprise then that the *Faith and Practice* of the Yearly Meeting was also undergoing revision and had been for some time prior to our arrival. As in SAYMA, the process had begun as an effort in part to bring "inclusivity" to the language of the guide, but the revision process soon became a lightning rod for everyone who wanted changes in the Society. My impression was that the majority of those serving on the revision committee were those who were interested in moving away from the traditional testimonies. The goal was not necessarily to approve in an explicit way *non*traditional practices or arrangements; it was merely to let the language of the guide "breathe" so that no Friend would feel "judged" or "excluded" by what was said there. The new mantra was that anything you believed or did was fine as long as it was "consensual," "nonexploitative," and "spirit-led" (whatever that now meant).

The rationale given for the proposed changes was the doctrine of "continuing revelation." Activist Friends argued that what the Spirit was saying *now,* in late twentieth-century America, was that people should be freer in personal matters than they traditionally had been. Women had a "right" to decide whether or not they would give birth to their unborn children. Adults had a "right" to engage in whatever kind of sex seemed good to them as long as there was mature consent and no intent to exploit. To deny individuals freedom in these things because the Scripture condemned such practices or the tradition of the Society forbade them was, revisionists argued, to set Scripture up as an "outward form" or set up "tradition" as an outward standard, thus denying the possibility that God's revelation could "continue" or change over time. There was a terrible momentum in the eighties for these demands, a momentum that made it very difficult for people to speak out honestly if they opposed the kinds of changes being advocated.

No one who was a Friend could deny that "continuing revelation" was a vital concept for Friends, but the relatively unbounded version of it current among Friends at this time was a far cry from what early Friends had meant by the term. In Barclay's explanation of it in his *Apology,* he was careful to assure his readers that such continuing revelation would never lead to utterly new and contradictory truths, and that the "established gospel and doctrines" would always be the foundation upon which new leadings would rest. This was what the discernment process was supposed to assure, but the discernment process had largely broken down.

The discernment issue had been the very thing my husband had been drawn to Friends to explore in the mid-1970s, and it was largely the discernment process that we two had struggled with in finding our own way through our tangle of old mistakes, difficult-to-govern impulses, and the new faith that we had come to through Friends. So it wasn't long before he became involved in the discernment struggle surrounding the revision process, especially as it had to do with attempts to change Friends' traditional sexual testimonies. I was concerned about it and followed it closely, but he was the one on the front-line of the struggle—going over the drafts that came out of the committee, explaining them to people in our Monthly Meeting, helping us to understand what they entailed, speaking out at Yearly Meeting, trying to dialogue with people supporting the changes about the concerns he had, and being a voice for those who did not want the changes but feared speaking out. He believed that the spiritual fruits of the sexual revolution had been destructive in ways people were not yet willing to acknowledge. He also believed that Friends could be convinced to approach the discernment process with spiritual integrity and not just bulldoze over obstacles in the tradition, whether they came from Scripture or from people in the Society who were not particularly enamored of Scripture but who still deeply believed in the old-fashioned sexual standards Friends had held to over the years. The struggle was prolonged and sometimes bitter. It was hard on him, and that made it hard on me. Over time it bred in me a sense of discouragement about the Society. My sense was that it was the theological divisions that existed among Friends that made any kind of ordered discernment impossible.

Incorporating a concept like "continuing revelation" into a religious tradition requires three things: a common starting place, a group discipline, and agreed-upon principles of discernment. For Friends, the starting place had always been the gospel of Christ as early Friends had articulated it and agreement as to the spiritual fruits such a gospel would bring forth in the believing community; the group discipline set forth in Friends' business practices; and the principles of discernment that had always included at least testing any new revelation against the Scriptures and then against the corporate judgment of the gathered community. But the process had broken down. The group discipline Friends had designed—its business procedures—were fairly well-adhered to, as was the principle of deference to the judgment of the group. But the two areas where the system had broken down concerned agreement as to the original vision, the starting point, and the principle that required the testing of new "revelation" against the revelation embodied in the Scriptures.

The status of the Scriptures had suffered terrible blows in the modern era, and Friends shared all the modern doubts about the Bible's apparent lack of reliable historicity, the "primitive" quality of the spirituality reflected in some of the writings, and the way some believers made sentences from them serve as simple proofs in arguments over complex issues. To these now was added the accusation of radical feminists that both the structure of ancient Jewish culture and the general mindset of the Scripture writers were tainted by patriarchal assumptions that were inherently oppressive to women. How could one refer people back to these writings to test modern leadings? If Scripture was as inherently problematic as alleged, then it really could not be used as an objective referent in the discernment process. But if one rejected the limited role Friends had prescribed for Scripture to play in their discernment process, there seemed no bridge at all for Friends back to the "established gospel and doctrines" that Barclay had assured us were central.

The other discernment "test," the only one that seemed to have any widespread acceptance in the Society—testing new revelation against the community's corporate judgment—seemed equally problematic to me given the lack of theological unity. How could you submit a leading to people when there was among them no common understanding of what "the established gospel and doctrines" of Friends were? The *forms* for testing leadings were there—the clearness committee process, the business process, the recorded past decisions the community had made—but the *real, common light* that needed to be focused on those leadings was missing. Some Friends thought of themselves as Christian, others did not; some did not even consider themselves to be "theistic." How could there be any corporate judgment when everyone cast such a different eye on things? The past documents adopted by Friends and recorded in minutes of past sessions were not a statement of the underlying "gospel and doctrines." They were simply statements made or decisions taken on specific issues at different times in the past.

But the problem went even deeper than this. Even the concept of "leadings" itself had become problematic, and nowhere was this more clear than in the disputes over sexual issues. A "leading" for Friends was a sense of the inner guidance of God on an issue or matter that one confronted. Early Friends' writings are full of references to such "leadings," "motions," "checks," or "pressings." What was the status of such a concept in the modern context? This was one of the most troubling things I saw in the modern gay-rights movement, the way it had of labeling its opponents' inward response to their lifestyle as "homophobic." "Homophobic" meant that you had what was described as a deep and abiding "revulsion" or resistance to the idea of homosexual sex. This approach to the issue bothered me and worried me because it was just such gut feelings—not passing or ephemeral or merely emotional, but inner convictions—that endured and could not be banished that were at the core of what Friends had always seen as God's "voice" in them. If you could be convinced that such a gut conviction was just some pathological antipathy or cultural conditioning, then how could any "motion" stand? Weren't these kinds of "motions" or feelings about moral situations what all Quaker leadings rested on? With these inner "checks" suspect, Scripture discredited, and unity of spiritual vision lacking, how could there be any kind of meaningful discernment?

Arguments over what the "fruits" of the new sexual ethic were or promised to be were also inconclusive. Proponents argued that the "bad" fruits that people pointed to—breakdown of family cohesiveness, adverse health consequences, chaotic lives, out-of-wedlock births, and abortion—were not *inherent* in the new vision they had.

In the end, the only discernment "check" that everyone agreed to go by was the check of Friends' established business procedures, the forms that even modern Friends agreed should rule when it came to deciding what we could or could not say as a community. The rules required that any change in official statements could only be made when there was "unity" among Friends at a business session called to discern what the community should do or say about something, and this unity was not there when it came to most of the issues activists wished to see addressed. It wasn't there when it came to the issues more traditional Friends wanted to see addressed either—the issue of abortion, for example, which some Friends thought should be part of our peace testimony. The past words and decisions of Friends, with all their limitations, stood for the most part since new words could not gain acceptance.

The struggle over the *Faith and Practice* was long and hard. It took a toll on everyone who engaged in it. In the end, no dramatic change was made in any of the traditional testimonies and practices of Friends, but the stresses were too great. It is one thing to be basically rooted in a common vision in which different people see different avenues arise. There can be disagreement and argument even where there is a fundamental, underlying unity of vision, but the stresses that arise from an underlying disagreement as to the foundational vision are very enervating. One begins to wonder the kinds of things early Friends wondered about the churches they were part of before becoming Friends. Where is the joy of the gospel? Where is the life in Christ in all this? The crucifixion is part of his life, but there is also resurrection. Where was that?

Outside these things, my husband and I had many good things happen in our lives outside of Meeting. The children were happy in their new home. Our family was blessed by the addition of a new child, an adopted son we believe came to us through God's grace as well. We were not granted a family rooted in biology, but we were amply provided with a family made whole and strong through faith. We continued doing some of the happier things we had done for years—having a Bible study in our home, meeting periodically with Christian Friends—with the hope that that these things would help us keep our sense of bearing and give encouragement to the efforts people were making to advance the propagation of early Friends' vision and the Christian gospel generally. But here too I began to feel a sense of frustration and concern as time went on.

Christians in the Society who felt silenced or judged or condemned as out of step with the latest crazes or movements sweeping through the society at large tried to gather strength and support by meeting together from time to time, but these gatherings seemed increasingly wounded and isolating as time went by. There was little joy or energy there, little sense of the power and largeness of Christ's Spirit that early Friends had recaptured in their gatherings. I wondered if I would ever know the peace of Christ's presence in a communal way, without tension or controversy or dispute. I began to wonder if I really was where God wanted me to be.

It wasn't just the weariness of battle over the issue of whether and to what extent Friends were meant to be followers and believers in Christ, though that must certainly have played its part. And it wasn't just the lack of joy and energy in the small community of Christian Friends that were trying to revive the Christ-centered faith of early Friends. It was more complicated than both these things together.

It started with a growing realization that the Society of Friends was laboring under a burden that was difficult if not impossible for it to avoid—the burden of sectarianism. Sectarianism in the sense I am using the word here means being bound too tightly to the religious vision or message of one individual or a small group of individuals. We Friends—Christian and non-Christian—were all very tied to the vision and practices that George Fox and his closest associates had articulated as "the gospel." The reform movement we were part of, New Foundation Fellowship, saw its role pretty narrowly as reviving Fox's christocentric vision as the cure we needed for our drift away from the "established gospel and doctrines." But our "opponents" were just as much wedded to Fox as we were. They didn't see his orthodoxy as central to his most profound insights. They saw his rejection of outward forms as more central, and his rejection of the historic church (and the Reformed churches of his day as well) as pretty much lost in apostasy. When we pointed out that Fox accepted the words of Scripture as God's words and something concrete against which leadings could be tested, they would counter with Fox's own words that the truths he proclaimed had come to him *without* the aid of any man or outward writing. If we argued that Friends had been in all respects believers in the major doctrines that defined the Christian religion, they would say that that was only happenstance, that no one in the seventeenth century had the analytical or intellectual tools needed to set Christianity aside and see into the universal pool of spiritual wisdom that later discoveries would make possible. Their "pariochialism" was unavoidable given the limits of human knowledge in the seventeenth century. They believed nevertheless that Fox's methodology—his distrust of outward formulas and forms—pointed in the right direction beyond the particulars of any denominational tradition.

The problem was that Fox had not seen the inward Christ he preached as an "aspect" of the gospel message the apostles were charged with preaching. For him, this Christ was the substance and totality of that message. Christ had come; the outward "types" and "figures" were forever a thing of the past. This was Fox's message. That other Christians did not see it this way made them apostate in his mind. That the church historically had not seen it this way made it apostate. If you accepted Fox as "the authority" and source of gospel truth, there was no way back to the larger church.

Fox's approach to the gospel had been beneficial in an environment where people were too much "caught up" in the outward aspects of religion, but modern Friends did not live in such an environment. Modern Friends, like modern people generally, were "caught up" in different things: secularism, relativism, individualism, and skepticism of all truth. If we wanted to call them off these things and back to Christ, we had to go beyond Fox. We had to get back to the outward things that Friends had thrown off. But this was just what Fox himself had made it impossible to do. Our "legitimacy" as Quakers rested on our relationship to Fox and early Friends, one way or another. That was our sectarian dilemma.

Paul warned members of the early church at Corinth about the dangers of tying oneself too closely to the human teachers who bring the gospel of Christ to the community. Even by the middle of the first century, the danger of factions and/or sects had become apparent. Even when he was one of the teachers to whom people tied themselves, Paul warned that our loyalty as Christians is never supposed to be to the people who bring us to Christ but only to Christ:

> What then is Apollos? What is Paul? Servants through whom you came to believe. . . . I planted, Apollos watered, but God gave the growth. . . .
>
> According to the grace of God given to me, like a skilled master builder I laid a foundation, and someone else is building on it. . . . For no one can lay any foundation other than the one that has been laid; and that foundation is Jesus Christ (1 Cor. 3:5–11).

The greatest irony for Friends is that this is precisely what Fox thought he was doing—getting people to look back to Christ rather than to the human teachers from whom they had gotten their religion. New Foundation people understood this, but they themselves could not get behind the man who had taught it to them.

Fox and his fellow Quakers saw in the historic church only a human institution, but my own experience and my own walk was teaching me to see it as something more.

10

What Did I Say?

Given the difficulties and questions that are inherent in the Quaker notion or doctrine of "continuing revelation," difficulties I have discussed at some length, it is not lightly that I turn now to the insights I came to feel that God was opening in me. The famous Fox quotation Friends used to capture the spirit of what continuing revelation was about—"You will say Christ sayeth this, and the apostles say this; but what canst thou say?"—was something I felt challenged by too.

What I came to see after some years as a believer and a Friend was that I was doing this same thing with the words and writings of early Friends that they criticized people for doing with the Scriptures. I was not paying as close attention or giving as much weight to the insights God was opening to me personally. What was it God was trying to open in me? What did I have to say about faith, about the redemption story I was part of, about the condition of the church, about the things God wanted us to deal with in our world—the kinds of things early Friends had been called upon to address in their day?

What ultimately got me to realize that I did have something to say was the teaching I had the opportunity to do beginning in 1985 and the encounter with Scripture that it forced me to. I was asked to take over the Quakerism course my husband had been teaching for a year or so in the Middle School of the Friends

School where he worked. Nothing clarifies like teaching. No matter how much you think you know about something, you never really know it until you learn to teach it—especially until you learn to teach it to the young. The point of the course was to teach seventh graders about the basic beliefs and values of Friends, such as why it was "unQuakerly" to be mean; why lying or cheating could easily get you expelled from the school; why we wanted students to dress simply and without eccentricity; why they were *never ever* permitted to wear army fatigues or military gear to school, even on Halloween; why we *never* permitted lotteries or chance drawings of any kind at school functions; why community service was such an important part of school life; and why we all sat in complete silence for thirty or forty minutes each week at the Meeting House on the off chance someone would have something to say "from the Spirit."

Had I been asked to teach adults, I would no doubt have gone straight to the Quaker texts I loved and have quoted so extensively in these chapters. But my students were only twelve years old, and most had had little exposure to religion of any kind. They would never be able to understand Fox or Penington or Barclay—a lot of adult Quakers had trouble with the seventeenth-century English they used, not to mention their theology. Since all of Friends' original beliefs and principles rested on biblical foundations, it made sense to use the Scriptures directly and to supplement them with my words to describe the way Friends had interpreted the critical texts. Something about just having to use my own words brought me into the concepts more, so that I really saw them in a clearer way.

There was also another reason why I wanted to use the Scripture "story" as my text. I had recently read a book by a man named Stanley Hauerwas—*The Peaceable Kingdom*—and I was taken by one of the ideas he introduced me to in that work. Hauerwas proposes in this book that Christians make moral decisions not by applying abstract principles to a situation, but by imagining themselves in the biblical narrative and making a judgment about what kind of decision or behavior seems consistent with the embedded principles of the people who are heroes in the narrative. Hauerwas is a moral theologian who teaches at Duke University, a Methodist much influenced by the outlook and testimonies of the Reformation peace churches. His interest in what I have since learned has a name—"narrative theology"—is directed primarily at the moral sense of direction the biblical narrative can provide to the believer. His approach to the biblical narrative was somewhat different from the approach early Friends had taken—seeing the general trajectory of the Scripture story as something that recapitulated itself in the spiritual life of the seeking person. But it seemed complementary to me and somewhat simpler to understand. It did not involve interiorizing the story or seeing things in terms of ministrations. Hauerwas's point was that the religious narrative in which our religious tradition was grounded functioned in the same way our other narratives do—our personal family narratives, for example, or our national narrative—to help us define who we are, what we stand for, and how we should behave in difficult situations.

Hauerwas's approach to the Scripture narrative was also useful because it permitted me to be neutral with respect to questions I could not really get into with my religiously diverse group of students: Were the Scriptures inspired by God? Were they inerrant? Were they authoritative? What was the correct way to interpret this passage or that? I didn't really need to get into any of these difficult questions. All I needed to do was familiarize them with the narrative and let them understand how Quakers saw it. I had read the Bible on and off for years and was familiar with all that Friends had said about it being a story that replicated itself, but I have to say that I never saw how much it does present itself as a narrative until I started teaching it. I actually remember the first day I stood up in class with the book and noticed out loud that the book begins at the beginning of time and ends at the end of time, and that it thus purports to deal with the entire history of God's creation. It startled me that the story presented itself as so utterly comprehensive.

I tried to look at the story without interpreting too much. I wanted the kids to see what Friends had seen there, but I also just wanted to see the story as it presented itself. For most of the story, the version of the story early Quakers saw seemed fairly convincing. Mankind is created by God to care for the creation and be "his image" in it, but man rebels against God's clear command to him and falls away from the closeness that was intended by God to exist between them. He doesn't physically die, but enters into a kind of spiritual death, which according to the story results in all kinds of misery and violence. The "fall" is thus the "problem" or "conflict" (as any English teacher will tell you, you must have conflict in a narrative) that propels the story forward and lays the foundation for God's continuing involvement in it—his efforts to redeem his work or bring it to the perfection he has intended from the beginning. It is to fulfill his original creative intent that God stays involved in human history, to bring man out of the death he has chosen into the fullness of life it was always God's intention for him to enjoy. It is crucial to man's identity as God's "image and likeness" and crucial to God's creative intent that the relationship of love and dependence God intended for man be entered into freely—thus the importance of "the test." The serpent is that power of evil in us and in the world that tempts us to choose things other than dependence on God. But there is a promise given early in the story that the "head of the serpent" will eventually be bruised (Gen. 3:15) by the "seed" or offspring of the woman—Eve—and one of the things the story will show is how trustworthy the promises of God are.

After the failure of the Noah project, God's redemptive work takes up with Abraham. God sees in Abraham a man who will listen to his voice and *do his will*—the archetype of the hearer and obeyer that is so central to Friends' understanding of faith. Out of the obedience of this one man will come a people who will hear and obey. The law and outward rites are given to this people to train them and guide them, but there is much backsliding and faithlessness. Error and repentance are thus part of the journey, as are the prophets God sends to reprove and guide the people back when they go astray. As the people mature in the context of God's redemption, more is expected of them—a deeper understanding of God's law, a more spiritual grasp of his will, and again it is the prophets who will help them come to these deeper understandings.

But the journey is not without deep and catastrophic setbacks. The division of the kingdom after Solomon and the many years of unfaithfulness and abuse under the kings who follow him ultimately lead to a near destruction of God's people and many years in exile from the Promised Land. In the midst of the suffering and turmoil brought on by these events, there is always the promise and hope of renewal and return. The prophets see a future Messiah who will heal the people of God, restore the kingdom promised to David, and bring a new covenant to man—one not written in stone or even in ink, but one written on the human heart so that even the promise of Eden, the home God intended for man from the beginning, might be restored.

In time, a man is born whose life and teaching lead some to believe that he is the promised Messiah, but it turns out he is both less and more than had been expected. He does not do all that they had come to expect the Messiah would do—he does not lead armies or depose the Roman occupiers. But after his death on the cross, his followers experience him resurrected and they come to believe that he is actually more than the Messiah. He is God in the form of man. They see in him the substance of all that God has previously brought forth from the beginning to draw people to him—the substance of the "types" and "figures" of the story in all their fullness: God's light and Word, the new Adam, the seed of Eve, man's offerings to God, the ark, the manna in the desert, the water from the rock, our scapegoat and sin offering, our priest, our shepherd, our prophet, our king, our law, and perhaps most of all, our new covenant.

The story goes on to say that Jesus leaves his disciples, telling them to baptize all people. The Holy Spirit comes and Christ's church is born. The church believes that Christ will return soon to end human history and gather his faithful to himself. But he does not return. We learn a little about the first decades of the church, but then the narrative ends, at least as history. The real end of the biblical narrative comes in the Revelation of John, which portrays in symbolic or imaginative terms what the end of history will be like. History, insofar as it has to do with the past, ends in the first century, biblically speaking. Quakers incorporated the Revelation part of the narrative by saying that events prefigured there could be experienced on a spiritual plane even though they had not yet come to pass, just as all the events of the narrative could be *inwardly* experienced. We could come into the full presence of God and sup at the great banquet in a spiritual way in this life. But Quakers did not see the historic events that unfolded after the establishment of the church, after Christ's ascension, as having much weight or spiritual significance. Like the New Testament writer of Hebrews, they saw

Christ's coming as the end of all outward types and shadows, the culmination and end of God's redemptive work in the world. They used the image of the sun and compared Christ's coming historically to the rising of the sun (Son) to its zenith over the earth. As the sun (Son) rises to its fullnness—to its zenith—it casts "shadows" in the world (the "types" or outward forms), but once it is "come" (or risen to its fullness), the shadows disappear and what you have is perfect fullness (what Friends called Substance), the fullness of God's Spirit and light.

This image spoke to me. It explained why Friends did not feel the need to see God's redemptive truths embodied in outward things like sacraments; but over time, it also led my mind to see what it was Quakerism did not address. The sun did not stop at noontide; it had a downward course to take as well to complete its story, and during this part of its course through our world, it would inevitably cast "shadows" again because the world it illuminated was just that way. It contained things that both obstructed and made real the sun's presence. This image, the sense of what it implied, the sense that it revealed something true to me about the course of the redemption story and the way God was working the world today, opened a way out of the labyrinth I felt Quaker theology had placed me in. It helped me see a way of resolving issues about the place of outward things in religion, the legitmacy of the historic church, and the matter of apostasy as well. I began to see another way the narrative could be viewed and other truths it might open.

I know this sounds strange. It is very hard to communicate how a vision of something comes to one, how a different way of orienting oneself to a story like the biblical story can open things, solve issues, or lead one in a direction not yet taken. It is very mysterious, but these insights brought me to some important conclusions and insights.

I realized that the Friends' "culminationist" way of seeing Christ—the idea that he ends history and the need for all outward religion—was something they came to because they were unwilling or unable to see that the real human history that came after him was part of the redemption story as well, the second half of the story, and that this second half might be meaningfully complex. In this they were like other Christians of their day, especially the Reformation Christians, who looked so exclusively to the biblical text and its first-century orientation. But the church had a life too; its history also mirrored or recapitulated the story of God's first people.

Friends had always assumed that the individual believer would go through something like a recapitulation of the Old Testament story in coming to God, but it apparently had never occurred to them that the church Christ started might itself go through such a recapitulation. But why not? The church was not just a human institution, a place that contained the truth within four walls like a bank has money. It was a living organism, the assembly of God's people, Christ's Body in the world. And if the in-gathering and shaping of the Jews as a people had taken two thousand years (and was in fact still going on), then how many millennia might it not take to gather in all the "nations" of the world formed as a people for God? How many challenges might that project involve? There would be times of faithfulness, but there might well also be times of scandal and disorder. The first people of God had known such times. Why should those gathered by Christ expect to fare better?

The story of God's first people was in the Scriptures. I am not saying it is history as we might write it today, or that it is all perfectly written or perfectly understandable, but its general line is comprehensible and instructive. It is a story of people who were bearers of a promise from God, who brought to the world an understanding of what it is to live lives consecrated and devoted to God and to God's purposes for man. What Christ did was to open that redemption to all; he revealed to all the depth and perfection of that redemption, but he did not end the story. He bestowed a promise on the leader of his disciples to bear that redemption forward in time. The assembly of people bearing that promise—the church—would not necessarily be any more perfect than his first people had been. They might even be so rebellious and unfaithful that God would be tempted to withdraw his promise from them, but there would always be enough of a remnant to go on. God's work among us was not over; he might still perform great works among his people that we cannot even imagine.

Coming into this vision of the story made it impossible for me to continue as a member of the Society of Friends. I felt I had to return in some way to the church that was connected to the apostolic promise.[1] For me, that meant bringing myself back into unity with the Catholic Church, which I saw as the bearer of Christ's promise and commission to Peter. For the second time in my life I felt the same pull. Everything else in the particulars of my story was different, but again I felt God's call to be there. I wasn't drawn back to it because I thought that they were the bank into which all truth was deposited. Sometimes Catholic converts who write their stories seem to see the Catholic Church in this way, but that is not my take on it. We are all broken, and we all share the blame for that brokenness. But the line of continuity still calls. There is no do-over for the church.

On the other hand, I do think the "do-over churches"—the Reformation churches and sects that arose in the sixteenth, seventeenth, and eighteenth centuries—articulated and lived out aspects of the gospel that the historic church, both Catholic and Orthodox, have not appreciated or developed as well as it should have. They have invaluable insights into the gospel Christ gave us.

Was this insight that grew in me from God? Was it nonsense? How could I ever know? I felt it very deeply and very powerfully. It squared with what I could understand of God's revelation in Scripture. It wasn't the kind of leading I could readily take to Meeting or even to Christian Friends; it seemed inappropriate for me to ask Friends if this vision of Friends' limitations and errors in theology might be something from God. So I talked to a priest. Things had changed in the years since I had left the Catholic Church. In 1964, when I had first sought membership in the Catholic Church, there had been a sense of rejoicing that I had found my way to the "one true church." But in 1987 they hardly seemed eager at all to see me return. God worked in other churches too. They seemed basically complacent with the brokenness that so exercised me.

My husband too had trouble understanding. He understood my frustrations; if anything, he felt them even more than I. The strain in him had been enormous. But he didn't see the Catholic Church as I did. He didn't hear God calling him to that different struggle. He still felt the call to keep to his witness among Friends. The thought that somehow the faith we had come to in so many ways together, as a team, would not be something we stayed together *in* was painful to both of us. We didn't really see things differently; I think we both saw the church (the universal church) as something that included both the Catholic Church and the Society of Friends and the evangelical churches as one, but that didn't change the fact that we saw our ministries differently.

I felt it was imperative for me to go back. It seemed to me also that the Catholic Church understood better than Friends and most other Christian denominations that Christ had not necessarily come to end outward forms and observances of religion, but to extend them in new ways that represented a real continuation of his physical presence among us. The sacramental spirituality of the Church and the outward letter of Scripture both perpetuated Christ's presence among us in necessary ways. The Scriptures give us the story we are part of and knowledge of who and what Christ is—at least an initial knowledge. The sacramental presence of Christ reminds us of his real presence in our midst in a way that transcends what even Scripture can give. The sacramental does not displace the inward—it introduces us to it, nourishes and guides it. Without it, the inward too easily becomes merely personal and subjective.

The outward dimension of religious faith is important—the principle ideas or "notions" that make up the Christian gospel, the information Scripture contains about the journey of redemption, about Christ, the apostolic preaching, and even post-apostolic understandings that the church came to through the workings of the Holy Spirit are all important—not because they are the "end" we seek, but because the spiritual dimension that is what we seek lays somehow behind or within them. This is the mystery of our existence as human beings, this interpenetration of outward and inward, this coexistence of matter and spirit. Early Friends had not bypassed the outward; they had penetrated it. That they *believed* they had bypassed it did not make it so. We who were dealing with the results of excluding it were in a better position to judge its necessity.

Still, while I felt it was a matter of some consequence that I return, I did not want to go back with the usual message about how messed up the Protestant churches were and how the Catholic Church was the answer to all the mess there was outside it. That was not it. There was a mess inside the Society of Friends, but that mess was not at the heart of the experience

Friends had given me. I had come into Christ among them. There was a dimension of the gospel they knew about that I had not found among Catholics, and this God did not want me to lose. This was the thing that I needed to offer up to the Church—a part of the "fullness of the gospel" that they saw as their job to protect and nurture. I still wanted very much to be a Christian after the manner of early Friends; I wanted to know Christ at the very center of my life in everything I did, and I did not feel a desperate need to partake of sacraments or do the kind of outward things that were so much a part of the Catholic religious culture.

Christ had begged his disciples to remain one in him, to be so completely one "that the world may believe that you [God] sent me [Jesus]" (John 17:23). We have not been faithful to him in this. We are now very much divided—perhaps not with as much hostility as in the past, but still very much divided and mostly over things that seemed increasingly meaningless. My own sense of it was that the Catholic Church came the closest to being the church that Christ had founded. It went back to apostolic times. It had a sense of itself as the bearer of Christ's promise to Peter that he would build his church on him and give him the keys to the kingdom (Matt. 16:18–19). It saw itself as charged with Peter's love of Christ and his charge to feed Christ's sheep (John 21:15–17). It was not only the promise bearer; it was also the spouse who had gone astray and become worldly and corrupt and unfaithful, the one God's wrath had been poured down on and scattered, just like the people of God's first promise.

Out of this jumble of insights, coming as they did against the backdrop of frustration and struggle I felt embroiled in as a Friend, ultimately came a sense of clarity, a sense that God was calling me to return to the Catholic Church. Indeed, even my sense of what it meant to be faithful *as a Quaker* seemed to require going back to the Church. When I talked with people about it, the responses I got were interesting. Curiously, most of the positive feedback I got came from Quaker friends. It was widely appreciated in Quaker circles that there were aspects of Quaker spirituality and Catholic spirituality that overlapped or coincided: the belief in Christ's "real presence," for example, or

Friends' notion of "continuing revelation," which is similar to the Catholic view of the developing tradition to which they attach such importance. There were also the mystical elements that were similar. One Quaker minister I knew actually admitted to me that he too sometimes mused over the idea that Quakers might really be considered a kind of religious order for lay people in a Catholic context. But among my other friends, especially those who were or had been Catholic, a sense of bafflement typically greeted my announcement that I was contemplating a return. How could I reconcile the antithetical approaches each took to worship and church order—the extravagant outwardness of Catholic religiosity with the utter inwardness of Friends; the authoritarian, hierarchical order of the Catholic Church versus the democratic and egalitarian order that reigned among Friends? Others wondered how I could possibly consider going back to a church that was so "antiwoman" and so "out of touch" with the needs of our time—population control, the need for changes in our sexual mores, and so on. One friend accused me of going back just for the security Catholic authoritarianism offered. My husband felt I was romanticizing the alleged "unity" the church had had in the early days and being completely unrealistic in thinking that it might ever attain such unity on this earth. None of this mattered in the end. God just wanted me to go back. I was sure.

Sometime in 1987, I began the process of normalizing my relationship with the Catholic Church. This involved sorting out the status of my first marriage, my divorce, and my remarriage as a Quaker. In 1988, I received what was called a "Declaration of Freedom," which recognized that my first marriage had not occurred in any kind of religious context and that I was free to enter into a second marriage in good standing with the Church, something I would need to do to be in full communion. In 1990, my husband and I remarried in the Church and I became a Catholic again. But I repeat, I did not go back because I thought the Church had everything right. I did not go back because I thought I would be completely satisfied with the Christian community I found there or the degree of faithfulness I would find among Catholics at large. I went back because I believed God wanted me to go back, and *as a Friend* I would have proved unfaithful had I failed to obey his voice.

11

Catholic Again

For me, being a Catholic means being in unity with the church that the apostles started, with the promise-bearing institution Christ charged with the mission of bringing God's redemption forward in history. It doesn't mean rejecting what I learned from Friends or the sense of God's continuous presence in my life that Friends brought me to see. To me, the truths the Catholic Church defends and the truths that I found among Friends represent the two necessary poles of the Christian gospel—the corporate and outward (or sacramental) pole on the one side and personal and inward pole on the other. These poles sometimes seem to be mutually exclusive and contradictory, but the truth is they are poles that need to be in constant contact and tension. It is the tension between them that makes the spiritual life dynamic—capable of stages, growth, and transformation.

As I mentioned in the previous chapter, there are areas where Quaker and Catholic spiritualities really do coincide, and I want to devote more time to developing how I think this is true. Of course, there are also areas where the differences are profound and where I have missed the "culture" of faith I enjoyed among Friends. I am constantly reminded inwardly that coming back was only part of the calling I felt as a Friend; the second part was that I bring to the Church the things I found among Friends that could enrich it even more. This, of course, has been far more challenging.

First the similarities. Both the Catholic Church and early Quakers believed that Christ was and is really and completely present in his church and among his people. He promised us that he would be "with us always, even until the very end of time" (Matt. 28:20), and he has kept his promise. For Friends, however, the Christ we can know and be joined with is only Spirit; but for Catholics he is also miraculously and mysteriously present in the sacramental dimension of the Church's existence—in the bread that is broken at Mass, in the priests who break the bread, in the Holy Father who tends the sheep and encourages the brethren, and in many other ways. I do not see why one necessarily excludes the other. Perhaps I am just not an "either/or" sort of person, but instead a "both/and" sort. This is the richness of the Trinitarian God we worship. He is Creator God, Christ, and Spirit, and each is an opening into the other, so there is no reason why he should be present to us only inwardly or only in sacrament or only in and through nature. He is in all of these. He is before us, beyond us, in us, in our church, in the bread he breaks for us, in the love he manifests to us in all these things. And when we join ourselves to him, we see him everywhere—in all these things and others besides.

His gift of himself in our communion bread is a very corporate presence; his gift of himself to us in our minds and hearts is very individual and personal. The relationship between inward and outward is infinitely complex—the outward stimulating and shaping the inward, the inward recognizing and infusing the outward with power far beyond what is there alone. If we were angels—beings whose essential nature was not tied to the physical creation but were in some way we cannot imagine purely spiritual—then perhaps the substance of the gospel could be that spiritual, "unclothed" essence some modern Friends take it to be, not bound up with time, history, concrete physical reality. But we are not angels. Our essential nature is bound to physicality, time, history, concrete mediating forms that are our ways into the world of spirit. When we try to pretend we are like angels, that we don't "need" outward things to mediate spiritual truth, we pull away from truth, come unmoored from the forms through which we came to the measure of truth we are capable of possessing.

Sacramental spirituality, in my estimate, is based on a better understanding of our human nature and ultimately on a better understanding of the wisdom of Scripture. It reflects the reality that we are part of the creation; that our comprehension of God is mixed up in a complex and mysterious way with the physical world that we are grounded in. We enter the dimension of spirit through physical doors. It is from behind these doors that our creator calls to us. We tap around these doors like blind men looking for him. It is our nature to tap and explore around them, God's grace working in us. If we are responsive to his call and persist in our seeking, the doors will start to open, revealing the deep truths that lie behind them, truths that give human life its meaning. At such moments we may be tempted to relegate the doors we passed through to something not so vital, to something that blocked or obscured the truths we now see more fully or more inwardly; but the doors we pass through are an essential part of the process of discovery. The sacraments are doors like this. They are physical but not solely physical. They are vehicles of that grace from God, who invites us to come through them to him.

Is it is possible for us to get caught up in the outward appearances and to forget that the doors must be gone through? I think it is. This is one of the dangers sacramental spirituality entails, but it is a danger we cannot obviate by doing away with sacraments. The shepherds who understand the power behind each door must take very seriously the task of keeping the sheep from thinking that the door is the ultimate goal. It is the proper place of the prophet to badger both sheep and shepherds, to scold them and maybe even sometimes threaten them so that they remain awake and moving spiritually. Life is short, and the rewards of coming through the door are much too great to give up on people.

The other question we must ask is, Is what lies beyond the door always exactly the same thing for every person who enters? If I experience my foretaste of God's kingdom as an intense intellectual pleasure at seeing the many parts of God's plan finding their fulfillment in Christ or in experiencing an almost excruciating sense of God's healing and redeeming love for his creation, or if I experience it in seeing my moral life transformed—not to perfection, but to a much higher state than my own will and my own understanding were ever able to effect in me—these are my experiences of God's saving power. Other people may experience God's reign over their lives differently. They may feel an overwhelming love and desire to emulate the life of Jesus without knowing much about how he fulfilled the promises made throughout the earlier stages of God's work in the shaping of the Jewish people. They may not have the capacity or the inclination to understand anything about doctrine or sacramentalism, and yet be filled with a kindness that has been shaped by God's love in a way I cannot understand. We ought not to have too narrow a sense of how God's saving power and love might be experienced by a person.

Another "Quaker notion" that can be found in Catholic spirituality is the idea of "continuing revelation." I have mentioned it several times. In a way, Catholics understood continuing revelation way before Quakers ever entered the scene. They simply called it tradition. Tradition and continuing revelation are grounded in the same belief—that God is not an artifact of history. He is as active today in the lives of his faithful as he was in the lives of the holy men and women of old, the ones we read about in the Bible. And he is active in the corporate life of his church, just as he was active in the creation of the universe, the history of his chosen people, and in the life of his Son. His wisdom is not confined to the Scriptures, though they are a product of his Spirit in a uniquely helpful way. But the men and women of Scripture are just men and women like us. God's Spirit led and opened truth to them, and it does to us as well—not everyone in the same measure, but everyone nevertheless. We could not know God at all unless we had his Spirit in us:

> these things [things that are part of God's wisdom] God has revealed to us through the Spirit; for the Spirit searches everything, even the depths of God (1 Cor. 2:10).

But continuing revelation is not just an individual phenomenon, not even mainly an individual phenomenon. It is primarily corporate. It is something the gathered people work out together over time, not something any one believer can definitively discern. When Christ promises that the Advocate will be sent to teach the disciples everything (John 14:26), it is possible to interpret this as applying to each one individually, but it makes most sense to see it as a promise that runs to the group, to the body they will become together. Clearly it did not take long for the church to hold that the guidance of the Holy Spirit Christ bestowed upon them belonged in some more reliable sense to the corporate body and in particular to its bishops than it did to individual members (not that individual members could not claim a measure of this same spiritual guidance). So when the church set out to discern truth in controversial areas such as the conflict between Hebrew and Hellenic Jews at the First Council of Jerusalem, it was a corporate task, not an individual one. Similarly, when controversy arose as to what writings Christians should look to as authoritative and which were to be given less weight, it was a council of the church that made the final judgment. That is how the Scriptures most Protestants take as solely authoritative came to be assembled and canonized. It is on the authority of the councils and the church that organized them that the authority of Scripture must rest in the last analysis. Had the church as an institution lacked the guidance of the Spirit, one could hardly argue that the judgments of the councils they called should be respected.

Early Friends, of course, rejected "tradition" as the Catholic Church defines it as something wholly of man, not of God; but in this it seems to me they were being inconsistent with their own insight. In a sense they were denying that the Spirit could ever have led the early church to organize itself as it did under the authority of bishops who were ordained and part of a continuing chain of leadership linking them to the apostles. Friends denied that the Spirit would ever have led the church to institute outward sacraments, creeds, and ordinances to keep the apostolic foundation secure. Friends saw "continuing revelation" as applying only to those gathered into their own particular vision of the church; the idea would have prospective validity only. The things the early church had decided were somehow not part of the chain of revelation, but still it is interesting to compare their approach to that of the Catholic Church. While both Catholics and Quakers hold that the Holy Spirit continues to inspire and work in his people and his church, both strongly insist that that any new revelation be consistent with the foundations laid by the apostles. Our God is not a God of confusion but a God of order, so claims of new insights must cohere with foundational teaching.

In the Catholic Church the right and duty of discernment on the issue of what new insights are consistent with the foundation belongs to the hierarchy, though in practice there is input from the grassroots. Among Friends, however, the right and duty of discernment with respect to "new insight into the established gospel" as Robert Barclay called it, devolves onto the membership as a whole. The interesting thing is that in both communities—Catholic and Quaker—the process of accepting new insights is very slow and methodical. In a properly functioning Meeting, changes in corporate testimony, while always theoretically possible, are as rare as they are in the Catholic Church. The rules established by early Friends require virtual unanimity to institute new practices or approaches. But when changes are convincing and a strong relationship to the gospel foundations are shown, the changes brought about under the doctrine of continuing revelation are impressive. Friends were among the first, if not the first, Christian group to forbid members in good standing to own slaves. They rejected the stigma of inferiority that attached to women in other Christian denominations and were among the first Christian groups to work against the death penalty. Their deep conviction that war and violence are inconsistent with Christian profession is widely known and respected. They also were among the first Christians to challenge class and race privilege as being similarly inconsistent with the gospel.

On the other hand, Friends did not and do not see the same "continuing revelation" in the observances and practices that developed in the early church to preserve and transmit what Catholics call "the deposit of faith"—that foundation to which Robert Barclay referred, on which the faith is built. They did not and do not see "continuing revelation" in the methods the church adopted to assure the soundness of the foundation or to meet the challenges of growth, persecution, and the deepening insights that came with both. But I think that the history of the Christian faith shows that these methods were also important for assuring that the gospel would survive in the world. Faith in the reality and need for continuing revelation brings change, but slow, respectful change. This is what I have seen among Friends at their best and in the Catholic Church at its best as well. The Catholic Church's past is just much longer and more complex than is that of Friends.

Yet another area of coincidence or common emphasis is one that is not often thought of by Friends, but it is nevertheless important. It is the belief that God's promises are foundational and trustworthy. When George Fox was a young man, seeking God and the power of God's redeeming work which had been so richly testified to in the New Testament Scriptures, he knew that if New Testament believers had experienced Christ's life and power, then he and his contemporaries should also be able to experience them. The promise of redemption offered through Christ was not a delusion or mere words. Friends continually used language that demonstrated how completely they believed they could rely upon Christ's promises to them. Likewise, the Catholic Church believes in the promises of Christ—in the promise made to Peter that he was the rock on which Christ's church would be founded (Matt. 16:19) and in the promise of the Holy Spirit's presence and power (John 14:26) to teach them and lead them into the fullness of truth. These are real promises, and like the promises to Abraham and to Moses, they are utterly trustworthy. Anyone who is brought into that inward experience of God of which Friends speak knows that the promises of God are palpably real and trustworthy, and this too strengthens my faith in the Church. The argument of the sixteenth- and seventeenth-century Reformers seemed to be that the Roman Catholic Church had departed so fundamentally from the holiness and faithfulness Christ had expected of them that they had forfeited their claim to the special status these promises seemed to carve out for them. I do think that in charging this and in shaking up the Church, they had a prophetic Word from God that the Church was meant to hear. But ultimately, I believe it was heard. If people believe that there are still things that need reform, they have a prophetic responsibility to speak what God gives them to say, but I think God is calling us to struggle over these things together, not to see imperfections as occasion to go off and be separate. The prophets of old did not leave and start their own communities. We should not either. It seems to me that the whole vision of and thirst for an eventual unity is missing in the Protestant denominations I am familiar with. People's identities are comfortably tied up in being Quakers or Presbyterians or Episcopalians. The Catholic Church is not perfect, but it still is the institution on which the promises rest.

The early months and even years of my return to the Catholic Church were not the easiest. The whole culture of the Church is different from the Protestant culture I had mostly known in my life—a different way of praying, of writing about Christ and his disciples, of talking about the faith, and especially a different way of conceiving of one's place in the community of faith. I don't think they are substantive differences, but they can get in the way of feeling at home. Asked to pray, a Catholic will almost always pray a set prayer like the "Our Father" or a "Hail Mary," while a Protestant will pray words that appear more personal and come to him or her in a more spontaneous way. The Catholic devotion to Mary caused me problems. I knew Catholics did not "worship" Mary or think of her as divine. I had little trouble with the reverence shown toward her as a person who opened herself to God utterly and completely, who permitted Christ to grow in her. These were virtues any Quaker believer could agree were modeled in her life. But the repetitious nature of the rosary went against certain Quaker ideas I had about how important it was for worship to be Spirit-led and spontaneous. And the frequent talk of visions of Mary, which are often encountered in Catholic circles, was something I could not relate to. But these were cultural differences, not theological issues for me.

The most disconcerting aspect of being back in the Catholic Church was the transition I had to go through from being a reasonably big fish in a little pond to being a tiny, virtually invisible fish in a huge sea. That is the way it felt. I don't mean to say I was a big fish in the sense that I was big and important. I wasn't. But in Quaker circles, people at least knew who I was. I served on committees that had a say in what went on in our Meeting. I taught First Day School, conducted Bible studies, did seminars at annual gatherings, wrote articles that were published by Quaker magazines. I taught Quakerism and even wrote a Quakerism curriculum that Friends bought and used in their Meetings or schools. If I went to larger Quaker gatherings, I knew people from all over the region—even all over the country. I felt that my voice could be heard. When I came back to the Catholic Church, I felt utterly anonymous. I knew no one. I had no place or position in the parish, no prospect of one. I had no Catholic "credentials" that could open opportunities. I could not see how "way would ever open" for me to do the other part of what I felt called to do, share what I had learned from Friends. I just had to be patient and wait for God to open the way for me in his time.

I needed to find ways of making the Church feel smaller to me on a day-to-day basis. It was not as easy as it might have been in a smaller denomination, or one more dedicated to creating social ties among its members. There was very little if any effort to do this in the parish to which I was connected, at least in the early 1990s. Eventually, however, things changed. I started to meet people and feel more a part of things. An adult study group started up in anticipation of the Jubilee year 2000, and it was a great success. Then I had the opportunity to stop my school teaching for a while and do the writing I felt God wanted me to do. So over time, the problem of being anonymous and part of a very large institution grew somewhat less important and less disconcerting.

Still, I missed the Society of Friends. As frustrating as I had found my life among Friends, I found I missed the Meeting for Worship—the simplicity of it, the freedom everyone had there to speak, and the sense I always had there of my life being really consecrated to God. I could and did visit fairly often and did not act at first to withdraw my membership from my old Meeting. To do this seemed inconsistent with my basic testimony that really what I was as a Friend and what I sought to be part of as a Catholic were aspects of one whole. But eventually I had to be dropped from the rolls. On a retreat once at a Jesuit-run retreat center in New Jersey, I had a poignant experience that reminded me that I had not returned to the Catholic Church to get away from the good things I had experienced as a Friend. In the intimate daily Mass we celebrated at the retreat center, the priest in charge had the practice of finishing his homily and then inviting all present to settle into a silence from which they could speak about the gospel readings if they felt moved to do so. In the silence that followed I had an intense experience of being visited by the Spirit and knew this was what I had come to find—

the Word in Scripture, in myself, and in the Eucharist. This was what worship could be—a blending of Catholic and Quaker practice that was so powerful I could not remember anything quite so right. Later on in prayer in the darkened chapel before the host, all alone, I experienced again the call to speak (or more specifically to sing). In the dark of the tiny chapel, I sang part of a Quaker song I had learned years earlier:

> I do not regret the troubles and doubts
> That I have journeyed through;
> They keep teaching me patience and humble
> devotion.
> Forget not in darkness what in the Light
> Ye knew to be the Truth.
>
> *Refrain:*
> Live up to the Light, the Light that thou hast;
> Live up to the Truth and remember my child,
> You are never alone, no never.
> Live up to the Light that thou hast,
> And more will be granted thee,
> Will be granted thee,
> Oh, live up to the Light thou hast.[1]

Then I just cried.

I would be remiss, however, if I did not also say that I was very pleasantly surprised at many of the wonderful things I experienced coming back. The first thing was the other side of the "little fish, big pond" problem I mentioned, for it wasn't all negative. The pond I was now in was huge. The number of people who went to Mass at my parish church each week exceeded the number of people I mingled with at a yearly meeting gatherings among Friends. The priests we had came from Ireland, India, and other countries as well. When I visited Israel in 1994 and attended Mass in Jerusalem, I worshiped with people from every continent and language group. We prayed in Latin, English, and French. The homily was given in Arabic and German (half and half). This was a church that was universal. And while among Catholics a far greater proportion of people participated in worship on what appeared to be a superficial level, there were also many holy and devoted men and women, men and women who had given up everything to devote themselves to the Church (in religious orders) and men and women who were deeply imbued with their faith as lay people. I came to love the diversity and universality of it. There were also forms of devotion and practice in the Church that were different from those I had come to know—particularly the kinds of simple devotion to and emulation of Jesus that mark some of the religious orders like Mother Teresa's Sisters, who live to serve the poor and seek Jesus' face in the faces of those who are dying or in need. This was one of the great blessings I encountered coming back, and it made me realize that faithfulness does include this serving dimension, a dimension I had resisted among Friends because it had been so politicized.

There have also been many blessings that I had not anticipated at all: a sense of deep appreciation for the sacraments and liturgy, for example, or the benefits I have found in simply reading the little prayer book I use, *Magnificat.*[2] Not all you pray has to be "yours" in the sense of being original. Christian believers are joined together in one body and we feed each other by the ministries we perform well. When I was going through the process of getting ready to return to communion, for example, I was not supposed to receive the Eucharist. It is a matter of some controversy among some that the Catholic Church restricts the taking of communion when you are not in full union or not in good standing with the Church, but I found it acceptable to be prevented. It seemed right to me that I submit myself to the rules and discipline of the Catholic Church I wanted to be part of, and I had learned as a Friend that rules and discipline are not extraneous to the health of the community. I found to my surprise that my Quaker orientation actually enriched the time of outward "deprivation" I went through. I found it meaningful that just before the reception of communion, everyone says, "Lord, I am not worthy to receive you, but only say the word and I shall be healed." These words, of course, are spoken in Scripture by a person who was not able to receive Jesus physically in his home. He was a centurion and a foreigner, and no Jew in good standing was supposed to enter into the house of a Gentile. But the whole point of the exchange between him and Jesus is to show that Jesus' physical presence is not the critical thing. The centurion's faith is. It is his faith that results in the healing of his servant, not Jesus' entry into his house (Matt. 8:5–13). That was my situation too. I couldn't receive Jesus into my "house" yet either, but I could and did receive him in faith.

Still, when I was able to receive him and participate in the liturgy fully, my outward participation also became full of meaning to me. Becoming a lector and being able to read the Holy Scriptures at Mass also became important. Many Protestants do not appreciate how substantively the Scriptures are part of the worship of the Church. Indeed, one of the things I came to appreciate about the Catholic Church was how perfectly its approach to Scripture paralleled the view I had come to take of it. They did not take a literal approach, but accepted it neverthelesss as authoritatively part of the teaching of the Holy Spirit. And they did not always "translate" it or interpret it. They stuck with the words they found there and left it open as to what the words might mean or lead to.[2] In fact, it surprised me how little this "authoritarian" institution actually did define what people should think of this or that Scripture passage—less than Friends had, that was for sure. In everything I participated in—liturgy, sacraments, retreats, Scripture groups, prayer books I used for daily reading, adult classes run through the parish—I felt fed in my spirit. Yes, there were controversies over modern-day issues—women's role in the church, sexual politics, even arguments over what I would call a Catholic form of sectarianism (the call to return to Latin and such other controversies)—but these things did not get in the way of real spiritual life.

But as much as I grew to love being back, as much as I came to appreciate the many benefits there were to being a Catholic, I knew I also had a burden on me to share what I had learned from Friends. This is ultimately the point of what I have written here, for I know that there are many contributions Friends' spirituality might make to the Catholic Church provided it is kept in touch and tension with the tradition the Church guards. It is to these I turn my attention now.

Quakerism offers in its approach to spirituality something all Christians might benefit from, especially Christians who have as rich an outward tradition as Catholics do. While it is true that Catholic churches in this country are well attended, it is also true that charismatic and evangelical churches all over America, not to mention Quaker Meetings, are filled with ex-Catholics who left the Church because they felt no encouragement there to go beyond the outward show of ceremony, sacrament, and dogma. There are also many Catholics who drift away from religion entirely. Part of why there are so many Catholics in these boats is because there are just a lot of Catholics. Many also stay in without ever feeling any deep spiritual reward from it. They stay because being a Catholic is simply part of the family culture. I don't mean to make it sound like a completely negative thing. It isn't. A person knowledgeable on some level with the gospel is, I think, more likely at some point to be brought into it at a deeper level, as the number of lapsed Catholics in other churches also tends to show. But it seems to me a shame that we in the Church do not do more to draw people into the deeper and more inward aspects of their faith. We all need a prophetic voice in our lives from time to time, and Friends' call to the inward Christ is such a voice to all Christians.

It also seems to me that there is a great hunger for inwardness among Catholics—both individually and in the corporate setting. I go on a regular basis to a Jesuit retreat center near my home. There is almost always some kind of Buddhist meditation going on, and I always wonder why we turn to traditions completely outside the Christian experience for this inward aspect when we have a sister tradition that focuses on that inward dimension the way Quakerism does. I do not know Buddhism or Buddhist meditation, and it would be foolish of me to say derogatory things about something I know nothing about, but Quakerism offers a rich resource to us from within our own spiritual tradition. The same is true of all the twelve-step groups that meet in Catholic retreat houses and churches. These all reflect a deep hunger among Catholics for a spiritual discipline or technique that can bring them into a more personal experience of God's saving power and life. But why do we always look abroad? Christ is in us, just as he is in our eucharistic bread. We can know him there, know his touch, know his guidance and his voice. We can experience his light and his judgment, his urgings and his comfort, and we can speak to each other what he opens to our hearts and minds.

Quaker spirituality also offers us a way to bring lay voices into our worship. The combining of Mass and Quaker-style worship that I experienced at the retreat center might offer a model of how such an opportunity might be opened to people; or perhaps Quaker-style meetings could take place in connection with reading Scripture apart from Mass, such as midweek meetings where people could reflect in silence on the ongoing presence of Christ's spirit and grace in their lives.

Quakerism (at least in its more traditional form) also offers believers a way of putting the Scriptures in a more central place. The catechism of the Catholic Church says that "ignorance of the scriptures is ignorance of Christ," but this has not quite filtered down as it needs to. Many Catholic homilists get bogged down in approaching the Scriptures in too scholarly or critical a way—almost as if they are worried that people will take them too literally or uncritically. But early Friends show us a way of using Scripture that does not require us to take them as literally true in every detail, but as writings that give us insight into spiritual truth. They see the Scriptures as the words God's Spirit brought forth through men to tell us what we need to know about God's existence and nature, God's intentions with respect to humanity's place in the creation, our relationship to him and to our fellow man, our spiritual condition, and the redemption God has worked to effect in history, including the extension of that redemption to all people in and through Christ. What difference does it make that some of these words of Scripture are literature, some history, some hymns of praise, and others letters or accounts putting the story of Christ in the context of the larger redemption narrative? The important thing for believers is that the Spirit of God gave these writings forth, gave them a unity and a power to reveal things about God and our spiritual condition that we could never know as reliably or as well without them. It seems to me also that a deep regard for the Scriptures is ultimately an implied acknowledgment that what the Church teaches about its own authority is true—that Christ's Spirit abides in it to guide it into all truth and make judgments about what is and is not part of his Truth, for the Scriptures rest on the legitimacy of the Church and its discerning judgment.

The Scriptures, however one analyses their weight and authority, are also where we have a degree of unity as Christians—Catholic, Protestant, and Orthodox. And they are where we have unity with the Jews, our "elder brothers" as Pope John

Paul II calls them, in the redemption God offers. It is through the language and framework offered by the Scriptures that we will ultimately find a common way of understanding and articulating our spiritual kinship.

Last but by no means least, Quaker spirituality offers lay men and women in the Church a way of seeing themselves and their lives as consecrated to Christ even without entering in to what the Church calls "religious life"—becoming a priest or nun or monk. One of the most serious drawbacks of Catholic Christianity for many Protestant Christians is the great divide that separates religious from lay members of the community. Quaker spirituality offers a tradition of lay holiness (though they would not call it that), a tradition of living in Christ's life and power in one's day-to-day affairs, that can be incorporated into our lives as Catholics. Christ offers to all believers his risen life for us to be part of. God wants us to hear him and follow him now, in this life. From the earliest chapters of our redemption story, God has called us to this:

> The Lord, your God, shall you follow, and him shall you fear; his commandment shall you observe, and his voice shall you heed, serving him and holding fast to him alone (Deut. 13:4–5).

> Then the people promised Joshua, "We will serve the Lord, our God, and obey his voice" (Josh. 24:24).

> Oh, that today you would hear his voice; Do not harden your hearts as at Meribah, as on the day of Massah in the desert (Ps. 95:7).

> This rather is what I commanded them: Listen to my voice; then I will be your God and you shall be my people (Jer. 7: 23).

> . . . the hour is coming and is now here when the dead will hear the voice of the Son of God, and those who hear will live (John 5:25).

> . . . the sheep hear his voice, as he calls his own sheep by name and leads them out . . . (John 10:3).

To live a life of hearing and obeying is something we can all commit ourselves to so that in everything we do we can "do rightly, justly, truly, holily, equally to all people in all things."[3] We can "live in the Power of Truth and wisdom of God, to answer the just Principle of God in all people upon the earth. And so answering . . . come to be as a city set upon a hill . . ."[4] There is no reason in the world why we Catholics ought not respond to the call to "let your lives preach."[5] I have often wondered why there is so little emphasis upon the idea of living consecrated lives among lay people in the Catholic Church; I don't know the answer except that perhaps the Church wants to let people know that it does not consider this level of commitment normative for everyone. Or perhaps there is a fear that a lay option will drain candidates away from the priesthood or the "religious life." But practicing the spirituality of early Friends is a way of consecrating one's life to Christ, a way that is open to any man or woman who chooses to put the hearing and obeying of Christ at the center of his or her life. Ultimately, offering lay people ways to deepen their spiritual lives can only improve the environment for vocations.

The other benefit in fostering among lay Catholics a knowledge of the kind of spirituality Friends developed is that it can provide people who must live in the world with the spiritual resources to avoid getting dragged down by that world. Quaker spirituality trains people to look at the world and its enthusiasms with discerning eyes, to live simple lives, to avoid materialism, insincerity, superficiality, and the allure of power. It teaches us to be patient, to see in small acts of integrity the path Jesus wants us to follow. And it teaches us that the life of Christ offered to us is something we can enter into today, in our lives here on earth.

But if we take to heart the deep and profound things Friends have to teach us, how can we be sure we will not also absorb their excesses? Perhaps one of the things that makes Buddhism attractive to some Catholics is that Buddhists do not threaten us as much. Buddhists don't have much to say about the things we claim to be and know. We will not find in their books passages comparing the Church to the whore of Babylon or the Beast in Revelation as we most certainly will find in some Quaker writings and Reformation writings generally. But I think we must learn to find a way to use the good in other Christian approaches without being threatened by the harsh things they might have said about us in their past anger and frustration. The prophets said some pretty hard things to the people of Israel, after all, yet they were not silenced or banished on that account—at least not forever. The Catholic Church needs to find a way of incorporating the prophetic voice Protestantism has to offer into its own larger story.

All I know is that Friends opened me to the God who led me back; and I know that the message I responded to is a message anyone can respond to, and I must remind my readers of it again before I close. The work of redemption God performed among the Jews and brought to us all in Christ is a work we are all invited to be joined to. Open your eyes and see that God is in you. He has been in you from the beginning. He has loved you, called you, guided you, lifted you up, and carried you. You have felt his work in you many times but have not seen him in it. Open your eyes and acknowledge him. Serve him, obey him, let his life grow up in you. If you do, you will experience a delight deeper than any you have every known, a depth of meaning in your life greater than you have ever imagined. As my friend Isaac Penington put it,

> I have met with my God, I have met with my Saviour; and he has not been present with me without his salvation, but I have felt the healings drip upon my soul from under his wings. I have met with the true knowledge, the knowledge of life, the living knowledge, the knowledge . . . which is life, and this has had the true virtue in it, which my soul has rejoiced in, in the presence of the Lord . . . I have met with the true birth, with the birth which is heir of the kingdom, and inherits the kingdom. . . . I have met with the true peace, the true righteousness, the true holiness, the true rest of the soul, the everlasting habitation, which the redeemed dwell in.[6]

Notes

Chapter 2

1. Woolman was a famous eighteenth-century Friend who led the Religious Society of Friends in America to forbid participation in the American slavery system to Friends. He predates the antislavery movement of the nineteenth century and articulates an unusual (for that time) faith in the equality of all people. He was also known for his strict simplicity and avoidance of "superfluities" in all things. He would have found it ironic that anyone would have been introduced to his thinking as a result of the outward appearance of his book.

2. Unless you count the memorial Meeting I held for him here after his death some thirty years later. My grandfather had no church, but he had liked our experience at the Meeting and felt fondly toward Friends for the good things I had found there.

3. T. S. Eliot, "Burnt Norton," in *Four Quartets* (New York: Harcourt Brace & Company, 1971).

Chapter 3

1. Eliot, "Burnt Norton," *Four Quartets,* II.62–65.

2. Ibid., V.137–143.

Chapter 4

1. Eliot, "East Coker," *Four Quartets*, III.123–126.

2. Francis Howgill, *Early Quaker Writings: 1650–1700,* Hugh Barbour and Arthur O. Roberts, eds. (Grand Rapids: Eerdmans, 1973), 176–177.

3. George Fox, *The Journal of George Fox,* rev. ed. by John L. Nickalls (London: London Yearly Meeting of the Religious Society of Friends, 1975), 14–15.

4. Convincement is the term early Friends used to describe their coming to see the reality of Christ's inward presence. It is different from conversion in the sense that it did not really involve an intellectual acceptance of the doctrines that made up Christian faith—they accepted these all along—as much as a "coming into" the power of Christ's presence inwardly.

5. Isaac Penington, *The Light Within and Selected Writings* (Philadelphia: The Tract Association of Friends, n.d.), 6.

6. Isaac Penington, *Early Quaker Writings,* Barbour and Roberts, eds., 233.

7. Eliot, "The Dry Salvages," *Four Quartets*, II.93–96.

8. Howgill, *Early Quaker Writings,* Barbour and Roberts, eds., 175–176.

9. Penington, *The Light Within,* 6.

10. Penington, *Early Quaker Writings,* Barbour and Roberts, eds., 233.

Chapter 5

1. Quoted in *Faith and Practice: The Book of Christian Discipline of the Yearly Meeting of the Religious Society of Friends* (Quakers) in Britain (1995), sec. 19:43.

2. Penington, *Early Quaker Writings,* Barbour and Roberts, eds., 239–240.

3. Fox, *Journal,* 7.

4. Ibid., 11.

5. Ibid., 8.

6. Ibid., 11.

7. The term "judaisers" was applied to those people in the early church who believed that the followers of Christ still needed to be circumcised and accept the Mosaic law. Fox expands its application to Christian leaders who insisted outward sacraments, priesthood, and liturgies were still necessary in the new covenant.

8. Fox, *Journal,* 107.

9. Howgill, *Early Quaker Writings,* Barbour and Roberts, eds., 179.

10. The Barbados Letter or statement basically goes through the major points of the Apostles' Creed and affirms the facts stated therein in an attempt to silence criticism of Friends' doctrinal orthodoxy. The letter appears on page 602–606 of Fox's *Journal.*

Chapter 6

1. Fox, *Journal,* 34.

2. Ibid., 31.

3. William Penn, *No Cross, No Crown* (Philadelphia: n.p., n.d.).

4. Fox, *Journal,* 16.

5. Charles Marshall, *Early Quaker Writings,* 82.

6. Howgill, *Early Quaker Writings,* Barbour and Roberts, eds., 177.

7. Fox, *Journal,* 4. This famous quote about people around him not possessing what they professed also shows that he too is in a state of confusion and despair, that he too does not possess the faith he professes.

8. Eliot, "Burnt Norton," *Four Quartets*, III.116.

9. George Fox, *The Pastoral Letters of George Fox,* T. Canby Jones, ed. (Richmond, Ind.: Friends United Press, 1989), 411.

10. Fox, *Journal,* 7.

11. Ibid., 15–16.

12. Ibid., 16–17.

13. In this, of course, he is like all of the New Testament writers and other early Christians who saw everything in the Old Testament as somehow relating to Christ. Fox is in this same general school of biblical interpretation.

14. Fox, *Journal,* 27.

15. Isaac Penington, *The Works of Isaac Penington* (Glenside, Penn.: Quaker Heritage Press, 1995), 1:64.

Chapter 7

1. Fox, *Letters*, 33.

2. Early Friends talked more of their "testimony," the whole living witness of their faith. But the values and behaviors that marked their corporate witness are typically referred to as "testimonies" today and have been for many years.

3. Penington, *Works* 1:367.

4. Fox, *Letters,* 273–274.

5. *Faith and Practice: The Book of Discipline of the New York Yearly Meeting of the Religious Society of Friends* (1998), 57.

6. "Unprogrammed Meetings" are those Friends' Meetings that retain the unpastored, unprogrammed form of worship developed by early Friends. In the United States, there are programmed or pastored Meetings as well.

7. Howgill, *Early Quaker Writings,* Barbour and Roberts, eds., 176.

8. Fox, *Letters,* 95–96.

9. Charles Marshall, *Early Quaker Writings,* Barbour and Roberts, eds., 81.

10. Fox, *Journal,* 37.

11. Fox, *Letters,* 154–155.

12. Fox, *Journal,* 667.

13. For an interesting discussion of Fox's approach to this issue, see H. Larry Ingle's excellent history of Fox entitled *First Among Friends* (New York: Oxford University Press), 161–194.

14. Fox, *Journal,* 65.

15. Fox, *Journal*, 399–400.

16. Fox, *Letters,* 45.

17. Yearly Meetings publish books called "guides" or "disciplines" usually called *Faith and Practice* that describe what Friends adhere to in general terms and the procedures they follow.

Chapter 8

1. Fox, *Journal,* 123.

2. Quoted in *Faith and Practice,* sec. 19:07.

3. Dean Freiday, ed., *Barclay's Apology in Modern English* (published through a grant from the Rebecca White Trust of the Monthly Meeting of Friends of Philadelphia, 1967), 63.

4. Fox, *Journal,* 399.

5. Nayler, *Early Quaker Writings*, Barbour and Roberts, eds., 109–110. There is an irony here, however, which should not go unmentioned. Nayler was one of the most promising of Fox's early followers. But only three years after writing these words, he himself faced severe censure (virtual rejection) by Fox and other Quaker leaders when he brought their movement into disrepute by engaging in a stupid display of "street theatre"—permitting himself to be greeted entering a town in the manner in which Christ had been greeted on entering Jerusalem with palms and praises of a bevy of female followers. The municipal authorities responded by charging him with blasphemy, a charge that resulted in his being pilloried, whipped, his tongue bored through with a hot iron, a "B" for blasphemer being branded on his forehead, and three years imprisonment. He was eventually accepted back into the Society and his writings continued to be held in esteem. Naylor's actions demonstrated the very difficulty we are exploring here.

6. Fox, *Letters,* 55.

Chapter 10

1. I realize that the Orthodox Church has the same claim as the Catholic to the kind of historical continuity that I have spoken of as being important to me. It is the promise to Peter that makes me see the Catholic Church as bearer of this promise.

Chapter 11

1. Lyrics are a portion of the song, LIVE UP TO THE LIGHT, by Susan Stark, PILCIR Productions, P. O. Box 804, Windsor Locks, Connecticut 06096. © 1977 Susan Stark Music. Used by Permission.

2. I am speaking here mostly of the Scripture that is incorporated into the prayers and liturgies of the Church, not the Scripture texts that are sometimes interpreted in the priest's homily. These texts are sometimes overinterpreted or deconstructed in ways I find unhelpful.

3. Fox, *Letters,* 154.

4. Ibid.

5. Ibid.

6. Penington, *Early Quaker Writings,* Barbour and Roberts, eds., 233–234.